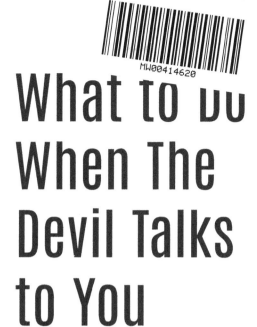

What to Do When The Devil Talks to You

How Christians
Learn to be Victorious
over Temptation

Dr. James Ford, Jr.

Urban Ministries, Inc.

FIRST UMI EDITION

Scripture from King James Version (KJV)

Published in the United States by Urban Ministries, Inc.
P.O. Box 436987
Chicago, IL 60643
www.urbanministries.com 1-800-860-8642

ISBN 978-1-68353-162-3 paperback
ISBN 978-1-68353-163-0 e-book

Library of Congress Control Number: 2017960891

Cover design by Laura Duffy
Book design by Astrid Lewis Reedy

Printed in the United States of America

Table of Contents

5
PREFACE

21
INTRODUCTION

1 **23** Listen to Jesus,
Your *Model*

5 **87** Listen to Jesus,
Your *Counselor*

2 **45** Listen to Jesus,
Your *Source*

6 **98** Listen to Jesus,
Your *Lord*

3 **63** Listen to Jesus,
Your *Teacher*

7 **109** Listen to Jesus,
Your *Strategist*

4 **78** Listen to Jesus,
Your *Historian*

8 **120** Listen to Jesus,
Your *Closer*

135
ABOUT THE AUTHOR

PREFACE

Let's play the antonym game. Think of an opposite for every word you see here. Ready?

Up
East
North
In
Good
God

Did you say "devil" on the last one? Hah! There is no opposite of God! Opposite implies an equality in two complementary or mutually exclusive things. Or, items moving away from each other at equal momentum. Nothing and no one is bigger than or equal to God.

Theologically, there's nothing good about the devil. He started well (Ezekiel 28:14). He was the anointed cherub that covered, from the Hebrew word *cakak*, meaning to overshadow. He was the highest ranking angel in heaven.

I have found three divisions of activity among angelic beings: *witness, worship, warfare.*

Examples of these three activities would be Gabriel, an archangel who announced the coming birth of John the Baptist to his father Zachariah (Luke 1). In warfare, Michael whom we find in Daniel 10 and 12, and Jude was an archangel. Over worship? Lucifer—son of the morning.

The highest-level activity on this planet is worship. The best thing we can do is worship Almighty God.

Lucifer used to be the choir director. He was the ultimate angel in heaven. But, imagine that he looked in the mirror: "Mirror, mirror, on the wall, who's the greatest of them all?" The mirror lied to him and he believed it.

In Isaiah 14, are the "I wills" to which God responds, "No, you won't." There is only one will in heaven—God's. So, he was kicked out of heaven. He was no longer Lucifer, but the devil—slanderer. The adversary. "The father of lies" (John 8:44). Theologically, there's nothing good about the devil.

"Ending" Times

While there is nothing good about the devil, there are strategies we can learn.

Revelation 12 kicks off the *beginning* of the end of the enemy of our souls. He is cast out of heaven. No longer does he have the access he had before.

Revelation 20 tells us about the *continuation* of his end. The archangel Michael comes and binds him in the abyss for 1000 years during the millennial reign of our Lord and Savior Jesus Christ.

Revelation 22 gives us the *culmination* of his end. He is cast into the eternal, infernal lake of fire. The devil is not the warden in hell. Hell was prepared for the devil and his angels. If you die and go to hell, it will be because you want to go. How do you *not* go? By asking Jesus Christ to be the Lord and Savior of your life. Jesus Christ is God, Who died, was buried and rose from the dead. As for the enemy of our souls:

Revelation 12
>His power is diminished (vv.9-11)
>His period of time is determined (v.12)
>His persecution is deterred (vv.13-14)
>His persistence is dogmatic (vv.15-17)
>His plans are defeated (v.16)

He knows it's over, but what lessons do we take away?
>1. **Perseverance**
>2. **Prioritize!**
>3. **Possibilities!**
>4. **Passion!**
>5. **Perspective**

1. PERSEVERANCE.

We must learn to hang in there. The devil never gives up. He takes advantage of every open opportunity. This passage in Revelation 12, is about him trying to destroy the genealogical line of Jesus Christ. He wanted to destroy Jesus. He wanted to destroy Israel. But he couldn't do it. And, yet, he keeps on trying. Again, he couldn't get Jesus, so he goes after Israel.

Think about this: whenever he fails, he intensifies his efforts. What do we do? A lot of us just give up. Look at verse 12: he has great wrath. In the earlier verses, it was simply wrath. Why? He knows he has a short time and therefore intensifies his efforts. He doesn't give up even though he's fighting a losing battle.

He doesn't have all that we have as incentives to keep fighting:

> **He doesn't have the indwelling Christ,**
> *But he doesn't give up*
> **He doesn't have the Bible,**
> *But he doesn't give up*
> **He doesn't have the Holy Spirit,**
> *But he doesn't give up*
> **He doesn't have angelic help of great magnitude,**
> *But he doesn't give up*
> **He doesn't have the promises of God,**
> *But he doesn't give up*
> **He doesn't have the anointing and power of God,**
> *But he doesn't give up*
> **He doesn't have the hope of heaven,**
> *But he doesn't give up*
> **His name is not written in the Lamb's Book of Life,**
> *But he doesn't give up*
> **He has no spiritual blessings in heavenly places,**
> *But he doesn't give up.*

We give up when we have much, much more than what the devil could ever hope for. How dare we do less than he does! We've giving up on that degree. Given up on that spouse. Given up on those children. Given up on that job. Given up on that ministry. Given up on that friend. Given up on that church.

We give up because it appears God hasn't done anything. But we must give God time! He's still an "on time God, yes, He is!" and, timing is everything.

Chef James

When I was young, my mother began teaching me how to cook. Yes, I can cook! I remember the first time she taught me how to fry chicken. She showed me how to season the chicken parts with spices and how to flour the chicken for frying. I was so proud. I heated the frying pan—she liked good ol' cast iron skillets.

Then she said, "Turn your fire down, son."

"Why, Mama?" I asked.

"When you put the chicken parts in there, the grease will be too hot and will cook your chicken on the outside too fast and the inside of the chicken will still be raw," she explained. Well, I didn't listen. I did it my way and sure enough, the inside of the chicken was undercooked and blood oozed.

"What happened?" I cried.

"I told you," she scolded me, "to turn your fire down so the chicken could cook all the way through. It takes time to fry chicken the right way, so that it will be cooked inside and outside."

And, isn't that some of us? We look good and well-done on the outside, but inside, we're just not ready—we're not done. For instance, there may be a call on your life to pastor. You preach a good sermon, but you don't know how to shepherd sheep. It takes time. Time to learn how people are and how to deal with them. You're raw. We can't "microwave" you.

> *And let us not be weary in well doing: for in due season*
> *we shall reap, if we faint not.*
> **Galatians 6:9**

A Tale of Two Frogs

Two frogs fell into a can of cream
So the story goes, I'm told
The can was shiny and steep
And the cream was really cold

"What's the use?" croaked Frog One
"Tis fate—no help's around.
"Good-bye my friend, good-bye sad world."
And weeping still, he drowned.

But Frog Two, made of sterner stuff
Dog-paddled in surprise,
While he wiped his creamy face
And wiped his creamy eyes.

"I'll swim around a while,"
I was told that's what he said.
"It really wouldn't help the world
"If one more frog were dead."

For an hour or two he kicked and swam,
And not once did he stop and mutter.
But he kicked and swam and swam and kicked
Then hopped out via butter!

Ode to Joy!

We know we need inspiration. A catalyst to help us persevere. What's the devil's motivation? He knows he's going to hell. He wants to take as many people with him as possible. What was Jesus' motivation?

> *Looking unto Jesus the Author and Finisher of our faith; who for the joy that was set before him endured the cross, despising the shame, and is set down at the right hand of the throne of God.*
> ***Hebrews 12:2***

Yes! It was for the joy that was to come of having obtained our salvation and His looking forward to eternal life with us. He looked beyond the *immediate* and saw the *ultimate*. Can you look beyond what you're going through and see to the day of completion?

In 2 Corinthians 4, there are seven reasons listed to help us understand why we can't give up:

The *privilege* of ministry (v.1)
The *proclamation* of the message (vv. 2-5)
The *perception* of the Master (v.6)
The *provisions* of God (vv. 7-9)
The **proper perspective** on suffering (vv.11-13)
The **power** of inner renewal (v. 17)
The **perspective** on the eternal (v.18)

Let's Hear It

A young man had made it all the way to eleventh grade and decided to drop out of high school.

"Son, don't do it," his dad tried to encourage him. "Son, ever heard of George Washington Carver?"

"Yes, Dad."

"He didn't give up. Harriet Tubman?"

"Yeah."

"She didn't give up. Booker T. Washington?"

"Yes, Dad."

"He didn't give up. Elmo McCremo?"

"No."

"That's because he gave up."

2. PRIORITIZE!

The devil keeps first things *first*! He prioritizes. He hates God and everybody and everything connected to God. Everybody who serves God. He couldn't get to God so after hitting earth, he goes after Adam through Eve.

What happens? God asks how it happened (although God already knew). Adam blames Eve, Eve blames the serpent and now the serpent doesn't have a leg to stand on.

Throughout Revelation 12, with the exception of verse 12, every verse begins with "And." That signifies that he is maximizing his time, is consistent and the action and response is continual. As his time decreases, his activity increases.

Monday is meeting day for my wife and myself. We talk about everything—finances, how much money she's spending… LOL!

Preface

In one of our conversations, I said to her, "Baby, I'll be turning sixty. If the Lord lets me live to see seventy, this is my decade of destiny. I have less time on this earth than I had before. I'm one day closer to my death today than I was yesterday. I have to maximize."

So I set some goals that demonstrate that I realize I don't have long on this earth. I want to write more books. I need to devote two hours a day to nothing but writing. I need to become a prayer warrior like my wife. I think I'm getting there. My wife made a comment one morning.

She said, "Now that's the first time I've heard you pray like that in a long time!"

I had to say to myself, *if you really believe this is your decade, what are you doing?* You know, when I was in the world, before I was saved, I didn't like "brown-nosers." Those who seek to please others. Folks would offer me help, time, and products but I wouldn't respond. But now, I ask, "How can this person help me accomplish my purpose?" Now I *do* call them.

Under Pressure

I found out Trinity Hospital was doing free kidney screening. Well, they had my middle name: FREE. I went and all I saw was elderly people, the youngest of whom had to have been seventy years old. I was tired of waiting and just as I put my hand on the door knob to leave, my name was called. This was God's timing.

This was a training session for student nurses. The young student who took my blood pressure said, "This can't be right."

She took it again. And again. And again. Finally, she called a supervising nurse who also took it.

"Girl, you didn't make a mistake!"

"What in the world are y'all talking about?" I asked.

"Sir, I don't want to alarm you, but your blood pressure is 254/167." She went and got the doctor. The doctor took my pressure. He agreed.

"You ladies are right." At this point, my heart is beating out of my chest! Of course, my pressure is up a couple *more* points. The doctor calls for an orderly to walk me to the emergency room with instructions to the ER doc on duty to put an IV in right away.

As we walked over to the ER, Bernard the orderly is talking to me trying to calm me down. I'm thinking, *dead man walking.* I started confessing my sins, your sins, the church's sins. I started confessing sins I hadn't committed—just to cover myself. Things I'd already repented of, I repented again! I was getting ready to meet Jesus! What else did I need to do?

It took a day and a half to get my pressure down to normal. Over the next few weeks, I was calling my kids and my wife EVERYDAY. There were things I was not going to waste time on. Time was short.

Time is short. We should be prioritizing. Jesus is soon to return. What're we going to do?

> *So teach us to number our days, that we may apply our hearts unto wisdom.*
> **Psalm 90:12**

But seek ye first the kingdom of God, and his righteousness;
and all these things shall be added unto you.
Matthew 6:33

3. POSSIBILITIES

And the earth helped the woman, and the earth opened
her mouth, and swallowed up the flood which the
dragon cast out of his mouth.

And the dragon was wroth with the woman, and went
to make war with the remnant of her seed, which
keep the commandments of God, and have the testimony
of Jesus Christ.
Revelation 12:16-17

Look at what the enemy is doing and note his creativity. He puts no limits on himself. He's willing to try something different. The old attack didn't work. For every attack, God responded with a counter attack.

Before I came to Christ, I used to play bid whist. I'm a very competitive person. Cutthroat! If you had an ace and I had a joker and I could trump you—BAM! I would slap that card on my head and let you see the book that was going to trump you.

That's what God did here. Everything the devil devised, God defeated. Notice: after he was dealt a defeat, he'd go another way. He uses kings, armies, people, nature, you name it. In the text that's given, he used five devices. The devil doesn't limit himself, he explores all possibilities. When will we take the limits off God? When will we take God out of the box and understand what God's word says?

Now unto him that is able to do
exceeding abundantly above all that we ask or think,
according to the power that worketh in us,

Unto him be glory in the church by Christ Jesus
throughout all ages, world without end.
Ephesians 3:20-21

When, again, will we take the limits off God? The enemy uses people. And, if he uses people it's because people let him use them. Is he using you? And, if he's in church, he had to ride with somebody. Did he ride with you?

What do we do? We refuse new ideas. We refuse to break with tradition. We're resistant to change. We're repulsed by the unfamiliar. We are safe and secure but we're stale and stagnant.

If you always do
What you've always done
Then you'll always get
What you always got
If you want something you never had
You've got to do something you've never done
—Jackie "Moms" Mabley

Ladies and gentlemen, if you want a miracle you've never had, you've got to do something you've never done: believe God.

Want something you've never had - good grades? *Study.*

Want something you've never had—friends? *Be friendly.*

Want something you've never had—good spouse? *Be a good spouse.*

In Matthew 4, after the devil is done tempting Jesus, he leaves—for a season. For a better opportunity. If he can't get in the front door, he'll try the back door. If not the back door, he goes for a window. If not the window, he'll come down the chimney. Not the chimney? He'll wait until you come outside. But, he will try to get in any way he can.

> *For a great door and effectual is opened unto me,*
> *and there are many adversaries.*
> *1 Corinthians 16:9*

Paul stated that a door of opportunity had been opened to him and there were foes. Whenever an opportunity is present, so are opponents. The opposition will always be as great as the opportunity. The question will be: how badly do you want this? There is pain in purpose. There is opposition in opportunity.

4. PASSION!

The devil is incapable of love. But he has passion in the form of hate. His hate intensifies. He's passionate about his hate. He does what he does because he's passionate about it. His hate is a driving force (Revelation 12:12,17). He never takes a vacation. Never calls in sick. Never takes a day off.

Mediocrity is the curse of the Christian walk. Lack of passion fuels mediocrity. Author Og Mandino stated in his book, *The Greatest Secret in the World,* that the *secret* is to "rise above mediocrity." Passion is a catalyst to that.

Do you remember why the Levites were given charge of the tabernacle even though they were not the firstborn?

> *Originally, the firstborn sons were to have been the priests of the Jewish nation, who would serve in the Tabernacle and in the Temple and be the spiritual leaders. When God spared the Jewish firstborn during the Plague of the Firstborn in Egypt, He "acquired" them and designated them for this special role.*
>
> *After the giving of the Torah on Mount Sinai, the Jewish people made and worshipped a golden calf. The only tribe that did not participate in this shameful act was the tribe of Levi. At this time, the firstborn lost their special status, and it was transferred to the Levites.*
>
> *In the Torah's description of the induction of the Levites as they began their new role (Numbers 8:16–18), God tells Moses: "For they [the Levites] are wholly given over to Me from among the children of Israel; instead of those that open the womb all the firstborn of Israel I have taken them for Myself . . ."*
>
> — ***Rochel Chein for Chabad.org***

The tribe of Reuben should have served based on their position as the firstborn. But Reuben lost his position after laying with his father's concubine (Genesis 35:22) and generations later, after the golden calf incident (Exodus 32). God honored the passion of the Levites for holiness rather than position, which the tribe of Reuben had lost generations ago.

Where's our passion for the things of God?

5. PERSPECTIVE

The devil has a global perspective. He wants to touch everyone everywhere. He wants to give everybody hell. He wants everybody to go to hell. Job 1 and 2—what was he doing? Roaming the earth. 1 Peter 5:8—doing what? Looking for people to devour—destroy.

Some of us aren't as good at being followers of Christ as the devil is at being the devil.

What shall we do? Don't give up. Keep first THINGS first—God and His Kingdom. Don't put limits on God or yourself. Serve God with all your heart. Touch as many lives as you can. That's what Jesus did.

> Jesus gave His **DIADEM** (crown) to His Father.
> Jesus gave His **DEITY** to humanity.
> Jesus gave His heavenly **HOME** up for an earthly home.
> Jesus gave His **BACK** to the Roman scourge.
> Jesus gave His **HEAD** to a crown of thorns.
> Jesus gave His **SIDE** to the spear.
> Jesus gave His **MOTHER** to John.
> Jesus gave His **LIFE** to the cross.
> Jesus gave His **BODY** to a borrowed tomb.
> Jesus gave His **SPIRIT** to the Father.
> Jesus gave **SALVATION** to all who receive Him.

Jesus is the giving God and we need to reciprocate. Here's a great example. One of the most giving people I've ever met asked me one day if I'd ever eaten at a particular Italian restaurant. I told him no, so he took me there.

As we entered, there was a homeless lady pushing a cart. She stopped us.

"I'm not a drug addict. My husband was. I lost my kids and all I own," she said. "I just want to get something to eat."

My friend reached into his pocket and said, "I knew God told me to get that $500 out of the bank for some reason." And he gave it to her!

The effect on me? I found myself being more generous. I found myself giving more. A man approached me and said he needed to go to his mom's funeral. He needed a tie. I gave him $50 and told him to get himself some clothes. I saw him a couple weeks later at Walgreens. He thanked me. He said he was so embarrassed to attend his mother's funeral. I told him, "Thank Jesus, Man!"

I see him in front of Walgreens often. I'm still witnessing to him. He said to me, "Man, everybody's always telling me about God. But you showed me God." People want to see God.

Last Story

The teacher offered a reward to the student who helped someone that week. The little boy who won had this story: his elderly neighbor across the street had lost his wife and was sitting on the porch weeping. The boy went across the street and sat with him—and cried with him. That's what people need. What we should be.

INTRODUCTION

There was a three-year-old boy named Johnny who lived in a small town in the Midwest. One day Johnny heard that the town would be having a parade. He was thrilled because he had never seen a parade before. Johnny's excitement grew even more when his parents told him it would pass right by their house. The big day finally came, and Johnny decided to watch the parade through a small knothole in the high wooden fence that surrounded his home. He peered through the knothole, but he could only see the bottoms of the floats as they slowly rolled past. As he continued looking, he thought to himself, "How boring and dull this parade is!" Suddenly, he heard a familiar voice say, "Come up here and look at the parade with us Johnny!" Johnny looked up and saw his parents calling to him from a second-story window. He quickly ran into the house to join them.

The spectacular scene that greeted Johnny's eyes both amazed and excited him. He could now see the whole parade from start to finish. He saw that the tops of the floats were adorned with colorful, bright and beautiful flowers. There were clowns of all sizes and shapes tumbling and somersaulting on top of the floats. Horses pranced majestically. Gaiety and splendor filled the street as the parade moved on. People with faces aglow lined the street. "Boy! What an exciting thing this parade turned out to be," thought Johnny. What made the difference in Johnny's opinion of the parade? The big difference was the position from which Johnny viewed it. His being able to see the whole show added a new dimension to it.

When it comes to temptation, we, like Johnny, must be able to grasp more than just the partial picture. We need to quit looking through the knothole of how temptation affects us through our present circumstances. The foundation for this panoramic view of temptation is illustrated for us in the account of Jesus' temptation in the wilderness. They are recorded in Matthew 4:1-11, and Luke 4:1-13. From these portions of Scripture, we can grasp the principles necessary to give us the proper perspectives to better understand temptation. They will not only enable us to view the completed picture but also know the primary characteristics of temptation.

This book by no means attempts to exhaust the subject of temptation but to merely supply a basic understanding so that the reader can have an overall view (God's) and not just a partial one (your own). It is my prayer that through the reading of this book you will gain perception, stability, joy, and victory while learning "What To Do When The Devil Talks To You."

1 Listen to Jesus, Your Model

Then was Jesus led up of the Spirit into the wilderness
to be tempted of the devil. And when he had fasted forty
days and forty nights, he was afterward an hungred.
And when the tempter came to him, he said,
If thou be the Son of God, command that
these stones be made bread.
But he answered and said, It is written,
Man shall not live by bread alone, but by every word that
proceedeth out of the mouth of God.
Then the devil taketh him up into the holy city, and
setteth him on a pinnacle of the temple, and saith unto
him, If thou be the Son of God, cast thyself down: for it is
written, He shall give his angels charge concerning thee:
and in their hands they shall bear thee up, lest at any
time thou dash thy foot against a stone.
Jesus said unto him, It is written again,
Thou shalt not tempt the Lord thy God.
Again, the devil taketh him up into an exceeding high
mountain, and sheweth him all the kingdoms of the
world, and the glory of them; And saith unto him,
All these things will I give thee,

if thou wilt fall down and worship me.
Then saith Jesus unto him, Get thee hence, Satan: for
it is written, Thou shalt worship the Lord thy God, and
him only shalt thou serve.
Then the devil leaveth him, and, behold, angels came
and ministered unto him.
Matthew 4:1-11

There hath no temptation taken you but such as is
common to man: but God is faithful, who will not suffer
you to be tempted above that ye are able; but will with the
temptation also make a way to escape,
that ye may be able to bear it.
1 Corinthians 10:13

Matthew records for us the temptation of our Lord and Savior Jesus Christ. What we'll see in this passage is the model Jesus set up for us to follow for those times when we, too, are tempted by the devil. At some point in time, all of us are tempted. If the devil had the audacity to tempt Jesus, who are you? Who am I?

We'll discover biblical principles for recognizing and dealing with temptation and exploring its very nature through the texts in Matthew and in 1 Corinthians. We'll also get an understanding about who the devil is and how he goes about tempting us.

Jesus Modeled the Message

Whenever Jesus gave a message, He modeled the message. Why? So that we can live out what we learn. For instance, in John 13-17, we have what's called the "Upper Room Discourse," which was Jesus' parting admonition and teaching for His disciples. Next to the crucifixion, this is one of the greatest examples of Jesus modeling His teaching for His disciples.

Imagine. The disciples are gathering for the Passover meal—the Last Supper—with Jesus. They've been walking the dusty streets and as the disciples walk into the upper room, they see a basin, a pitcher of water and a towel. It was standard hospitality to wash the feet of your guests. This was normally done by the lowest servant, the youngest child or in the absence of either, the wife. What they do not see right now, is the servant or the young child who will wash their feet.

Peter looks around. "Well, I've got the keys to the Kingdom. I'm not washing anybody's feet," he says. Of course, we know that means he was head of the deacon board!

And then, Andrew, Peter's brother, comes in. He sees the setup and remembers how Peter's feet used to smell, making his sandals all smelly after a day of fishing and resolves, "I'm not washin' *anybody's* feet!"

Thomas came in saw everything and said, "I doubt it!"

Judas arrived and said, "Well, I'm the treasurer and I'm not doin' anything." Treasurer means he was head of the trustee board.

Earlier, Jesus had just given His disciples a lesson on being servant leaders. "We're not over them and we're not under them. We're among them," He said (Mark 10). The one who would be the greatest of all must be the servant of all—a servant leader. Now Jesus turns around in John 13 and models what He just taught them.

They're all reclining around the table and the Lord Jesus Christ is bringing up the rear. At first, He's at the table reclining with them having supper. When supper is finished and Judas has gone his way to betray Him, Jesus gets up, removes and lays his garments to the side and wraps himself in a towel—like a slave. He then pours water into the basin and proceeds to wash the feet of the disciples. They are dumbfounded. But He is setting an example for His disciples and Jesus is setting an example for *us*. God is washing feet.

THE PRINCIPLE THING.

The question is still in debate today: was the temptation of Jesus real? Could Jesus be tempted? The *Doctrine Of Implicare* says that Jesus cannot sin. He didn't have a sin nature. Some say Jesus could not serve as an example for us *because* He couldn't be tempted—He was God. But whatever Jesus did while He was on the earth, He did not do out of His deity. He did it out of His humanity. Had He acted out of His deity—His Godship—it would not have counted. So, let's see just what the Lord Jesus Christ did in His humanity in order to overcome the evil one, thus giving us principles and a model to follow. Jesus overcame the devil by:

1. Recognizing Vulnerability *After* the Victory.

What had just happened? We have the attestation of the Trinity about the deity of Jesus Christ in Matthew 3. The Father identifies the Son as deity (Matthew 3:13). "The Son" is a designation of deity. Says Hebrews 1:8:

"But unto the Son he saith, Thy throne, O God, is for ever and ever: a sceptre of righteousness is the sceptre of thy kingdom."

Next, the Holy Spirit confirms this by descending on Jesus like a dove during His water baptism. This is the victory. What happens after the victory? The devil comes to tempt Jesus right after the victory. Look out for yourself after the victory. After the victory, we are most vulnerable.

Remember Elijah (1 Kings18)? He beats out 450 prophets of Baal. What a victory! But, what happens after that? He runs from one woman—Jezebel. Watch yourself *after* the victory.

How about Peter? Who is Jesus? "You are the Christ... the Mashiyach, the Anointed of God," (Matthew 16:16).

"I'm going to the cross," says Jesus.

"Not so, Lord!" Peter replies. An oxymoron. You can't say "not so" if you say "Lord." Amen? Watch yourself *after* the victory.

2. Realizing That God Allowed It.

The Bible says that Jesus was led up of the Spirit into the wilderness "to be tempted of the devil" (Matthew 4:1). Luke 4:1 states that Jesus was full of the Spirit as He was led into the wilderness. Now we discover that temptation is dual-faceted. The word for "tempted" here is the Greek—*peirazo*. The use of the word depends on the context. The devil's intent was malicious—to disprove Jesus' deity by causing His fall through temptation. God's intent was to prove Jesus' character and steadfastness of faith and obedience. In either case, God allowed it.

See the difference in motive and intent on God's part and the devil's part:

The Devil: tempts us
God: tests us
The Devil: make us stumble
God: make us stand
The Devil: break us down
God: build us up
The Devil: find our faults
God: fix our faith
The Devil: destroy our witness
God: develop our witness
The Devil: sin against Christ
God: shine for Christ
The Devil: pervert our walk
God: purify our walk

When we look at Job 1 and 2 for instance, we discover that the devil has a restraining order placed on him. It's the same when he approaches you or me. Peter says that we are a "peculiar people." The Greek word is *peripoiesis*, meaning "protected, preserved and under ownership." In this case, we are owned by God as His own treasure. There is a hedge of protection around us. There was a hedge of protection around Job.

Remember, God actually pointed Job out. The devil wasn't even thinking about Job until God pointed him out.

The enemy acknowledged to God, "You have a hedge of protection around Job and nothing can get to him unless You allow it."

So, God said, "Okay, I'll allow it." Of course, with all that God allowed, we know that Job passed the test and we praise God for that.

3. Replenishing Power - Be Filled with the Spirit.

Luke 4:14 says that Jesus returned to Galilee full of the Holy Ghost after the devil left Him. Ephesians 5:18 leads off the fact that it is impossible to live the Christian life without being filled with the Spirit of God. This is the hinge on which that door swings. There are no options here. Paul works his way through the other verses that follow, admonishing us that we can't:

> **Worship** without being filled with the Spirit (v.19)
> **Pray** effectively without being filled with the Spirit (v.20)
> **Submit** mutually without being filled with the Spirit (v.21)
> **Submit** to husbands properly without being filled
> with the Spirit (v.22)
> **Love** wives properly without being filled with the Spirit (v.25)
> **Raise** children properly without being Spirit-filled (6:1)
> **Relate** properly at work without being Spirit-filled
> **Defeat** the devil without being Spirit-filled (Ephesians 6:10-18)

4. Resisting the Devil's Appeals

Matthew 4:1-11 is a powerful passage that also helps us to understand the lust of the eyes, the lust of the flesh and the pride of life. Again, the devil came at the Lord Jesus Christ the same way he comes at us:

He attacked the physical **WEAKNESS** of Christ
resulting from 40 days of fasting (v.2)
He attacked the **WILL** of Christ
to prove Himself the Son of God (v.3)
He attacked the **WANTS** of Christ
to accomplish His mission without suffering (v.3b)

So, the enemy of our souls attacks us through our *appetites*, our *ambitions* and our *avarice*. Christ successfully fended off all these elements of temptation through the Word of God, knowing God and knowing Who He Himself was—indeed, the Son of God!

5. Relinquishing First Place to God

Every one of those temptations was an appeal to Christ's humanity and He disregarded each because He was seeking *first* the kingdom of God and His righteousness, knowing that all these things would be added to Him (Matthew 6:33). As we go after God's kingship in our lives, He promises that any and everything we'll ever need will be added to us. Not to worry.

6. Refusing to Entertain the Temptation

Jesus used the Word of God to answer the enemy. He didn't argue with him. He said what God had already said in the Word. He didn't "weigh His options." With the second temptation, the enemy interjected, "for it is written." The enemy will come at you with the Word. Herein is the importance of Bible reading and Bible study. The third temptation was to offer Jesus what He would ultimately get anyway—this planet—dominion of this world and its system.

He was offered what seemed to be a shortcut. The other route was the cross. Jesus chose the cross. He chose God's *will*, God's *way*.

7. Receiving God's Ministry

After the season of temptation was over, the Father released angels to minister to Jesus. And He was again filled with the Holy Spirit and power, entering into Galilee. The people who'd been waiting in darkness could now receive the Light of the World.

After soldiers have fought for a period of time in a war, there comes a time of R&R—Rest and Relaxation. A time to receive things that help take away stress and the side effects of having been in conflict. God, likewise provides us with what we need to de-stress after spiritual warfare.

8. Remembering, the Devil Never Gives Up

The devil left him, but would be looking for a more opportune time. Until we reach heaven, we will be challenged by the enemy of our souls—maliciously, going for our downfall. On God's part, temptation is allowed in order to strengthen our character and our faith. And the boundaries are set by God. He is faithful and will not allow us to be tempted beyond what we, by His grace, can handle.

DESIRE PLUS OPPORTUNITY

Now, let's take another look at 1 Corinthians 10:13:

*There hath no temptation taken you but such as is
common to man: but God is faithful, who will not suffer
you to be tempted above that ye are able; but will with
the temptation also make a way to escape,
that ye may be able to bear it.*

There are important principles here that dovetail with the Matthew passage. Can I tell you a story about being broadsided by temptation?

There was a new preacher in town—Pastor Brown. He was an old-school preacher. He went around the neighborhood knocking on doors and ringing bells to introduce himself and invite the neighbors to church.

As folks opened their doors, he began, "Hello, I'm Pastor Brown, the new pastor of the Baptist church right up the street and---" before he could finish, people would exclaim: "Nat King Cole! It's Nat King Cole!"

It happened over and over. He couldn't convince them otherwise. And then he knocked on a door that was answered by a woman in a slinky, come-hither outfit. She was "hood" sexy like Keyshia Cole. Movin' like Shakira. She had a face like Meagan Good. Body like Beyoncé. Eyes like Alicia Keyes. Voice like Whitney Houston. Personality—uhh—just like my wife.

He introduced himself: "I'm Pastor Brown."

She said, "Nat King Cole!"

Pastor Brown began to sing, "Chestnuts roasting on an open fire..."

So, what does it take for temptation to be effective? It takes desire and opportunity.

Desire + **Opportunity** = **Temptation**
Desire + **No Opportunity** ≠ **Temptation**
No Desire + **Opportunity** ≠ **Temptation**

Ever hear people give their testimonies of victory over what they never had a desire for in the first place?

"Pastor, Pastor! I got a testimony!"

"What's your testimony?"

"Well, this guy tried to step to me and I told him, 'Talk to the hand—my soul don't understand! I already got a man! His name is Jesus!'"

My question is this: you're giving me your testimony about somebody you didn't want in the first place. Do you have a testimony about someone you *did* want? If you had no desire, there's no temptation and therefore ... no testimony. Someone else has a testimony about never having been tempted to drink alcohol. Wonderful! But he never had desire to drink. Celibate? Yay! But that's not by choice! You just haven't had an opportunity ... yet!

My point: it's easy to have victory over what you don't want. If you don't want somebody, you have no desire even if the opportunity is there.

Can I tell you another story? My wife and I were at the *Taste of Chicago*. My wife spotted a guy whose pants were unzipped.

"Honey," she said to me, "tell that guy he's unzipped."

I said, "No."

"Well, I can't tell him. I mean it's really OPEN."

"NO."

"Now, Preacher, you should really be the one to tell him-"

"So I said, "Okay," and walked over to him. "Sir, excuse me, but you need to zip up."

"Oh, thank you for noticing," his smile was an invitation, sending the message of opportunity. There was no desire on my part - ever. No temptation.

How about Halle Berry? Man! Well, you may have the desire, but you'll never have the opportunity! Seriously, though, we have to be careful. When we have a desire and opportunity comes along, we can become mesmerized like a deer caught in temptation's headlights.

Just think: how many times have you said, "I'll never do *that* again," and find yourself doing whatever it was over and over again?

"I'll never lie again," and discovered that a lie was a very present help in the time of trouble? Or, cheating? How do we deal with it?

No Harm, No Foul

What Matthew teaches us is this: to be tempted is not sin. How do we know that right off the bat? BECAUSE JESUS WAS TEMPTED. The Bible says:

> *For we have not an high priest which cannot be touched with the feeling of our infirmities; but was in all points tempted like as we are, yet without sin.*
> **Hebrews 4:15**

Now, again, if Jesus could be tempted and He was—without sin—then temptation is not sin. The sin comes when we yield to the temptation. The hardest thing to *not* do sometimes is the very thing that we *want* to do. Like I say all the time—I wouldn't be tempted if temptation weren't so tempting.

WE'RE ALL IN THIS TOGETHER!

> *Wherefore let him that thinketh he standeth take heed lest he fall. There hath no temptation taken you but such as is common to man: but God is faithful, who will not suffer you to be tempted above that ye are able; but will with the temptation also make a way to escape, that ye may be able to bear it.*
> **1 Corinthians 10:12-13**

There are principles embedded in this passage that we must keep in mind and never forget in order to stay on top of things:

1. No Exceptions

There are no exceptions from temptations. Word to the *super saints*. A classic example is my man Pete. In Matthew 26: 33–35, Jesus tells Peter, "You will deny me." Peter looks around at the others and swears, "Though all of them deny You, Jesus, I never will." He throws them under the bus. And Jesus tells Peter that before the cock crows twice, he will deny Him three times. We know what happened. Listen. Often, we're most vulnerable when we think we're the strongest. We don't take proper precautions.

What's your reaction or response when a believer falls? "But for the grace of God, there go I?" OR, "That's a crying shame! How could he do that and be a believer?" Be careful!

Roll Call!

As we look at Scripture, we discover a lot of people who fell, not in the area of their weakness, but in the area of their strength. What would they say to us?

Noah—My strength was discipline. For 120 years, I preached and built that ark to specs. I went off the strength of what God said for 120 years. I blew it after the ark landed. Got me some *Champipple* and got drunk.

Abraham—My strength was obedience. I messed up by following my father instead of my heavenly Father. I went to Haran (which means "delayed") and was there five years. And God was silent. Because when we don't listen to God, God stops speaking...until we're ready to listen. And, God allows us to go through whatever it is that caused us to stop listening so that we won't want that to happen again and instead, we'll listen to God.

David—My strength was integrity. I was a man after God's own heart. I had sex with a woman who was someone else's wife. I tried to trick her husband into having sex with her to cover up the fact that I'd gotten her pregnant. He wouldn't, so I had him murdered. I did repent, but my family suffered for my sins.

Elijah—My strength was my faith. After God showed up on Carmel and set the altar ablaze, dealt with 450 prophets of Baal and His people, I heard Jezebel was after me. I ran scared. I became afraid of Jezebel and forgot Who God was.

Uzziah—My strength is adherence to God's Word. But, I got beside myself and went into the temple to sacrifice, which only a priest should do. I wound up with leprosy.

Isaac—My strength was truth telling. And then I lied. Told people my wife was my sister and she wasn't. I figured Dad got away with it, so could I. I was wrong.

Moses—My strength was meekness. And then I got mad and disobeyed God by striking the rock for water instead of speaking to it. Those people had worked my last nerve (and I only had one left!). I missed entering the Promised Land with the others. I saw it. I just couldn't go in there.

Peter—My strength is courage. What makes the muskrat guard his musk? Courage! Oops! Wrong story! I told Jesus I would stick with Him no matter what. I tried to defend Him in the Garden of Gethsemane. You know what He told me? "Put your sword away." He wouldn't defend Himself. I wasn't going down like that—without a fight. Some of the servants identified me. The third time I was asked if I were with Jesus, I started cussin' up a storm. Said I didn't know Him. And then, the cock crowed...just like He said. He turned and looked at me. I'll never forget that look ...

TIMELESS TRUTH

An unguarded strength is a double weakness.

CHINESE PROVERB

Never Say "Never!"

Jill Briscoe, the wife of Dr. Stuart Briscoe recounts a conversation with a neighbor on fidelity—being faithful to her husband.

"I'd never cheat on my husband," the friend stated, "Never! What about you, Jill?"

"Well, I'd hope the Lord would give me strength not to," Jill replied.

"Oh, Jill! You would never do that!"

"Well, I'll never say 'never' because you never know."

"Well, I'm going on record that it'll never happen," the neighbor retorted.

"What if it were a King David—a handsome man with power and looks..."

"Not even David! It'll never happen!" Later, the neighbor moved away. A few years later, Jill got a letter in the mail. The letter simply said, "Dear Jill, Call me. King David has moved in next door..."

Never say what you *won't* do. Proverbs 16:18 reminds us that pride goes before destruction and a haughty spirit goes before a fall. Looking at ourselves as believers, again, none of us are exempt from temptation. Like Peter, some of us speak too soon, brag too much, pray too little and think too late. Always ending up in a pickle because of "it."

2. No Escape

Temptation is "common to man." Paul is saying that temptation is the human dilemma. Everybody is tempted by something at some time, even though we are not tempted by the same things as others. We all have our proclivities. We need to know who we are. We need to be on guard.

We are not alone. We will never have an experience that millions of others have not already had. Circumstances may differ, but the temptations do not. Remember the three areas under which all temptations come: lust of the eyes, lust of the flesh and the pride of life.

It was in those three areas that Jesus was tempted in the wilderness. He was asked to prove His Sonship by turning stones to bread (lust of the flesh). He was tempted to show off and throw Himself down from the pinnacle of the temple (pride of life). He was offered the kingdoms of the world in exchange for worship (lust of the eyes).

The Root of the Problem

> *Genesis 3:6 –*
> *The woman saw that the tree was good for food*
> **(lust of the flesh)**, *and that it was pleasant to the eyes*
> **(lust of the eyes)**, *and a tree to be desired to make one*
> *wise* **(pride of life)**

Genesis 13 –
And Lot lifted up his eyes **(lust of the eyes)** *... it was well
watered everywhere* **(lust of the flesh)** *... even as the
garden of the Lord, like the land of Egypt* **(pride of life)**...

Judges 14:1-2 –
And Samson went down to Timnath, and saw a woman
(lust of the eyes) *in Timnath of the daughters of the
Philistines* **(pride of life)**. *And he came up, and told his
father and his mother, and said, I have seen a woman
in Timnath of the daughters of the Philistines: now
therefore get her for me to wife* **(lust of the flesh)**.

2 Samuel 11:1-3 –
*And it came to pass, after the year was expired, at the
time when kings go forth to battle, that David sent Joab,
and his servants with him, and all Israel; and they
destroyed the children of Ammon, and besieged Rabbah.
But David tarried still at Jerusalem* **(pride of life)**.
*And it came to pass in an eveningtide, that David arose
from off his bed, and walked upon the roof of the king's
house: and from the roof he saw a woman washing
herself* **(lust of the eyes)**; *and
the woman was very beautiful to look upon.
And David sent and enquired after the woman* **(lust
of the flesh)**. *And one said, Is not this Bathsheba, the
daughter of Eliam, the wife of Uriah the Hittite?*

David knew who she was: the wife of one of his officers, the
daughter of one of his men and the granddaughter of one of
his counselors.

Note in each case, it was lust of the eyes, lust of the flesh
and pride of life all the way through. The *root* of the problem

will always be those three things. Through Christ's example and the empowerment of the Holy Spirit by the grace of God, we can overcome temptation.

Bloom Where You're Planted

What do we see in Jesus' wilderness experience that the Holy Spirit enables us to imitate?

Submission to the will of the Father
(Philippians 2:5-7)

Show Satan's schemes
(Ephesians 6:10-12)

Sets an example for us
(Philippians 2:8-9)

Sympathetic as our High Priest
(Hebrews 4:15)

Shines for God
(2 Peter 1:17)

We know from what has already been stated that Jesus was led into this experience by God the Father for a reason. God will never permit such an experience without reason. We may not understand at the time, but the thing is to trust God. It's okay to ask questions. And expect answers, which will help us stay submitted. In the meantime, like Joseph, let's bloom where we're planted.

We've seen three constant areas that are the proven roots of every temptation: lust of the eyes, lust of the flesh and the pride of life. The method of employing these devices are varied, but the root can be identified and we know who's behind it.

We saw Jesus get through by saying what God said in His Word. We must do the same. Read and study and live and speak God's Word. Faith comes by His Word.

Because we know what Jesus went through, we understand that when we pray, we have a High Priest who sympathizes with us and that He genuinely cares because He's "been there." Our prayers are more trusting, because we know He knows. And we can count on the answer and help we need.

Jesus was also a witness for the Lord in all He did and said. He modeled that for us so that we could do the same. The world is watching us and we are to shine with the love, the power and the victory that comes from submission to God's will and an overcoming life. In overcoming temptation, we glorify God. We don't have to listen or yield to temptation.

3. No Excuses

We have no excuses for succumbing to temptation. God is faithful and has an escape route ready—if we are willing to take the escape route, unlike Adam and Eve who fell into temptation when the devil:

> *CALLED* their attention to sin—a beautiful tree (lust of the eyes)
>
> *CAUSED* their attraction to sin—the tree could make them wise (pride of life)
>
> *CAPTURED* their affection to sin and to settle for it—(lust of the flesh)
>
> *CORRUPTS* their ambition in sin—they would now serve it

COVER UP through hiding and blame—they discover the truth and the consequences of submitting to temptation rather than trusting God's Word

We don't fight *for* victory, we fight *from* victory. Our victory comes through our relationship with Jesus Christ. We sin not because we have to, but because we *want* to. We have to let the Holy Spirit change our *wanter*, so that what we wanted to do, we don't want to do anymore. We can't resist the devil if we're sleeping with him.

4. No Exploitation

God will not allow us to be tempted above what we're able to withstand. God will make a way of escape. If we are exploited by the devil it's because we want to be exploited.

We know the three enemies: the world, the flesh and the devil. But we have ammunition for our spiritual six-shooters:

> We *faith* the world—1 John 5:4
> We *flee* the flesh—2 Timothy 2:22
> We *fight* the devil—James 4:7

We overcome the world by faith. We don't fight the flesh, we flee it. Joseph learned that it's better to lose your coat than to lose your character (Genesis 39). We fight the devil through resistance. In all, fight the good fight of faith. Hang onto Jesus. We have a faithful Savior Who was fully human, but was the fullness of the Godhead bodily (Colossians 2:9). He understands our issues by His experience and can fix them by His Godship.

If there is a tragedy, it is for those who go to church but are not the *Church*. Those in church but not in Christ. Those who believe their salvation is wrapped up in a baptismal pool or membership roll, when it must be wrapped up in the Person of our Lord and Savior Jesus Christ. He is the fullness of the Godhead bodily (Colossians 2:9) and we are complete in Him. Jesus *is* our victory!

2 Listen to Jesus, Your Source

A TEMPTING OFFER

A guy was on his way to an important engagement and could not find a parking space. He parked illegally and left a note in case a police officer happened by and he rushed off. A police officer *did* come and was about to write a ticket when he saw the note. He removed the note held by the windshield wiper, which read:

> *Dear Officer,*
> *I was late for an important meeting and could not find a parking space. Please forgive me my trespass.*

The officer responded with a note of his own:

> *Dear Driver,*
> *Could lose my job if I don't ticket your car, so please ...*
> *lead us not into temptation.*

Ever notice that we don't have to *find* temptation? Temptation will find us! How is it that opportunity only knocks once, but temptation will beat your door down? Most of the time the devil is not going to bring anything to us that we don't like. So, how do I fight what I like?

We promised ourselves we wouldn't fall for some old tired line again, but we did. We liked what we were listening to. The person feeding us those lines could talk a starving dog off a meat truck. We went for it. We fell for it—again. We promised we wouldn't gossip anymore, but find ourselves hitting speed dial because we just had to "share" our concern about this juicy news at Christ Bible Church. After all, it was about the Pastor. I said I was going to lose some weight and can't believe I ate the whole thing!

> *I can resist everything but temptation.*
> OSCAR WILDE

THE NATURE OF TEMPTATION

Let's recap the first chapter so we can move forward. We saw some things concerning the very nature of temptation as we observed Jesus being tempted:

Temptation is not **sin.**

Temptation is not **selective.**

Temptation is not to be **sought.**

Temptation is not **single-faceted.**

At the root of *all* temptation is one or more of these three elements:

> *Lust of the eyes*
> *Lust of the flesh*
> *Pride of life*

Temptation is powered by two things:
Desire and Opportunity

Temptation is common to everyone:

> **NO EXEMPTIONS**—everyone is tempted. Warning to the super Christians: don't let your halo become your noose. We're all susceptible.
> **NO ESCAPE**—the enemy tempted Jesus, he can tempt us.
> **NO EXCUSES**—God is faithful to not allow temptation to be overwhelming and will provide an escape route. But we *must* take the escape route provided.

James 1:12-16 makes it clear that all sin begins with the condition of the heart. James talks about the process from temptation to the actual expression of sin:

> **INCEPTION** of sin:
> An idea is presented (v.13)
> **DECEPTION** of sin:
> A lie is embraced (v.14)
> **RECEPTION** of sin
> The invitation is accepted (v.15a)
> **CONCEPTION** of sin:
> Death is born (v.15b)

> ## TIMELESS TRUTH
>
> *We can't help what we see,*
> *But we can help what we look at.*
> *We can't help what we hear,*
> *But we can help what we listen to.*

It's a big mistake in thinking that the best way to overcome temptation is to just yield to it. The struggle is over—just give in. That thought seems to be driving some governments' policies and laws. Sweden legalized drug use rather than continue to fight it. Did it work? Employee time and work quality is down, healthcare costs are up.

Sometimes the hardest thing to do is to *not* do what you want to do. Story time. A little boy was staring at the apple bin in front of the grocer's. Pete the grocer comes out and asks, "Are you thinking about stealing one of my apples?"

"No," the boy replies, "I'm trying *not* to steal one!"

From the last chapter, we also want to remember that we deal with temptation by doing what Jesus did:
   1. ***Recognizing*** *Vulnerability After The Victory.*
   2. ***Realizing*** *That God Has Allowed It.*
   3. ***Replenishing*** *Power by Being Filled With the Spirit.*
   4. ***Resisting*** *the Devil's Appeals.*

God is in Control

Farther down the road at the end of His earthly ministry when Jesus was arrested and brought in on trumped-up charges,

He remained for the most part, silent. Jesus said very little to the High Priest and He said very little to Pilate. In fact, Pilate flexes his judicial muscles and in essence says to Jesus, "Don't you know who I am? I have the power to release you," to which Jesus replies, "You have no power except what's been given to you from heaven. So the person who sent Me to you has the greater sin" (John 19:11). Everyone was under God's sovereignty in terms of what they could do and how far they could go.

God has a restraining order on the devil and he can't do anything without God's say-so. As we think about this, it should change the dynamics of our thinking on trials, tests and temptations and ultimately, how we deal with temptation. Rather than say, "Why me?" say, "What are You trying to teach me, Lord?"

Again, Jesus as our model, teaches us what it means to submit to the will of the Father. Why is it significant that Jesus faces this challenge in the wilderness? What is the Father accomplishing here? Jesus is the Second Adam (1 Corinthians 15). Through His sacrifice, obedience and submission to the will of the Father, He is fulfilling and putting right what the first Adam failed at in the Garden of Eden. Succeeding generations failed at correcting it.

Paradise Lost

Paradise was lost under the first Adam. Paradise is restored under the Second Adam. The first Adam succumbed to temptation. The Second Adam overcame temptation. In the beginning, God gave man three things: work, Word and a wife.

The work and the Word comes before the wife so that Adam could be the spiritual leader and supplier of needs in this new God-ordained concept called "family."

Adam, by default, also had the responsibility of communicating to his wife, the Word he'd received from God. At the end of Genesis 2, all is well. By Genesis 3, the devil is talking to Eve—the wife. As you know, women are voice-activated. They like to talk. They are moved by what they hear. Adam stopped talking and the devil started talking—to Eve. Guys, just for the record, if you don't talk to your wife, some snake will.

In verse 6, a question comes up about the Word that was given by God. Eve gets into a conversation with the devil and misquotes God. There are two possibilities here. Adam didn't relay God's message to Eve exactly as it had been given to him (2:16-17). Or, Eve heard what Adam said, but she didn't *listen* to what Adam said (3:2-3). God said nothing about "touching" the fruit, but God *did* say that if they ate, they would "surely die." Eve had left out the "surely" part.

We discover in Genesis 3:6 that while this conversation was taking place, her husband was standing right there! Adam was *with* her! He never said a mumbling word! The wimp! He got us in all this trouble! He didn't speak up! He ate too! So, what happened? They failed the test.

Now along comes the Second Adam—Jesus Christ. He's not in a beautiful garden with docile animals. He's in the wilderness. Mark says that Jesus is in the wilderness with wild beasts (1:13). This Second Adam demonstrates that we can totally submit to the will of God. We can say, "No!" to our *appetites*, our *ambitions* and our *avarice*.

Partnering with Jesus

This was set up to help us understand that we can't do this alone. "What are you talking about, Pastor Ford?" Well, why couldn't Jesus just come one weekend and just die? Why did He have to live 33½ years on this planet? The Bible tells us this: Jesus died for our *justification*, but He lives for our *sanctification*. Now, the life we live in the flesh is not based on how we live it, but on how Christ *lived* it.

Stay with me, it all ties together. In this we learn and understand that Jesus was not just a model for victory over temptation, but we also get victory is *through* Jesus Christ. I can't overcome this, but Jesus already did—on my behalf. Therefore, once again, we don't fight *for* victory, we fight *from* victory because of Jesus Christ Who has already overcome (John 16:33) and defeated the devil.

Now, what we have is fellowship with Jesus, and the life that we now live in the flesh, we live through the faith of the Son of God Who loved us and gave Himself for us. Hook up with Jesus and stay hooked up!

Another story for you, to help illustrate this. The big event was coming up, a guy was going up against the champ in a boxing match. The purse was $1,000,000. Fight night has come. He's in the ring. First round, the champ knocks him down but he gets back up. Second round, the champ knocks him down again and again, he gets back up. Third round—same thing. All the way to the last round. In the last round, he KOs the champ! He wins!

Later, he arrives home and greets his wife. She never watches his fights because she can't stand the violence. He pulls out the belt and the check.

"Baby, I won!" he says, smiling. "Undisputed champion!"

"Honey," she says, "put that belt around me." He did. "Now gimme that check." He does.

"Baby, you are a conqueror," she smiled, "but I'm *more* than a conqueror!"

I like that. You know why? Because that's exactly what happened for you and me. Jesus got in the ring with the reigning champ—the devil, who'd deceived and stolen everything from Adam and Eve. When Adam and Eve blew it in the Garden, they relinquished the title deed to this planet, which belonged to them—to the enemy. The Bible said he was the prince of the power of the air (Ephesians 2:2). But, Jesus said, "Prepare Me a body and I will go down and show them how to live for You" (Hebrews 10:5).

Jesus comes along and gets in the ring—BAM!! The devil tried to knock Him out when he worked through King Herod to kill Him and all the baby boys in Bethlehem. When people of His hometown tried to throw Him off a cliff (Luke 4:28-30) and other times. But Jesus got up each time. In the final round at Calvary, the Lord Jesus Christ KO'd him and it was over!

Now Jesus Christ is the undisputed Champion of the world. The Bible says that God has highly exalted Him and given Him a name above *every* name (Philippians 2:9). Guess what?

At the sound of that name—JESUS!—every knee is destined to bow and every tongue will confess that Jesus Christ is Lord of all! On that day, the term "atheist" will be obsolete.

Then He took that belt and came to my house at 7372 Fermosa Way in Pittsburg, Pennsylvania, and put the belt of salvation around me. "I AM the Conqueror!" He declared. He gave me a check from Ephesians 1:3 made out in the amount of "all spiritual blessings in heavenly places in Christ."

"I AM the Conqueror, but now you are *more* than a conqueror through Him that loved *you!*" That's what this is all about. I don't fight him in my own power. But, I have a big brother... That's right! I'll put my big brother on you and you don't want to mess with Him! Even the archangel Michael didn't get up in his face—he said, "The Lord rebuke you!" (Jude 9).

Jesus be a Fence

As many know, I come from a "small" family of ten—nine boys, one tomboy (my sister). I was the oldest. The problem with being the oldest is not having an older brother to run to. But, I tell you, I got into more fights... You know why? My sister and my brothers went around telling folks they had a big brother! That's when I learned how to negotiate! I wasn't going to fight all those people! "Let's talk about this."

I used to push drugs. Ray, the guy who led me to Christ shared this with me: "You're a believer now. Let me tell you the best way to know that you're truly saved. You're going to see things that will make you say, 'Now, if I weren't a Christian that would have never happened.'"

Two days later, there was a knock on the door. It was my boy Soup (yeah, there was a name thing). Guess what he had? An ounce of reefer. Now Soup never got anybody high. He was one of those who didn't get you high, but was always around when you got high.

"I got an ounce, let's smoke." I thought, *now that wouldn't have happened if I hadn't been a Christian.*

I was on a bus, going from East Liberty to Homewood in Pittsburgh. I saw a woman I'd been trying to "step to" forever. She'd blow me off every time. But now, it was, "Hey, Bo." She came and sat next to me. "You know," she said, "I've been thinking about you lately." Again, I thought to myself, *now that wouldn't have happened if I weren't a Christian!*

She began talking about how I'd always wanted to get with her. Guess what? I got off the bus early—like fourteen or fifteen blocks before my stop. I thought to myself, *let me do what I'm supposed to do. Let me run!* She looked good. She sounded good. But I knew, she was sent by the devil.

And she was one of his devices. He knows what we like and he will hook you up! He knows you like them tall. He knows you like them bald with an earring in one ear. He knows you like "baby got back!" He knows you like that intellectual woman—the one who can articulate and pontificate. He knows you like the ones with money.

It is Written

When the devil issued a challenge, Jesus' reply was, "It is written." When Jesus said, "It is written," during His temptation, what He was saying in the original language was: "It was written in the past and it hasn't changed. It still stands today. And when Ford preaches it in the twenty-first century on this, there will never be a *new and improved version.*" Aren't you glad that God's Word doesn't have an expiration date?

> *The grass withereth and the flower fadeth;*
> *but the word of our God shall stand forever.*
> **Isaiah 40:8**

> *So shall my word be that goeth forth out of my mouth:*
> *it shall not return unto me void, but it shall accomplish*
> *that which I please, and it shall prosper in the thing*
> *whereto I sent it.*
> **Isaiah 55:11**

So when the devil comes, hit him with the Book! That's what Jesus did—God in the flesh. But He set an example for humanity.

I Feel for You...

We have a sympathetic High Priest. Jesus is able to relate to us by His experience on earth. Because we know what Jesus went through, we can pray with confidence knowing that He not only knows—He cares.

Homeless?

> *And Jesus said unto him, Foxes have holes, and birds of*
> *the air have nests; but the Son of man hath not where to*
> *lay his head.*
> **Luke 9:58**

Betrayed?
> *Yea, mine own familiar friend, in whom I trusted, which did eat of my bread, hath lifted up his heel against me.*
> **Psalm 41:9**

Instead of running *from* Jesus, run *to* Him. He understands and He is willing and able to do what is necessary to bring us victory in every situation.

I love my grandchildren to pieces. So wonderful! You know what's really wonderful? You can always send them home. Couldn't do that with children. But grandchildren... Folks tell me I've softened up in my old age. But, occasionally, I have to "get those legs." The first time I got Naomi's legs, she acted as if she would die. She sobbed uncontrollably.

"You still love me?" she asked.

"Yep."

"Then hold me," she reached up for me. I picked her up and held her. Then I started crying.

God said, "Teaching moment. You do wrong. You know I'm Holy. And, you leave Me. Prone to wander. I feel it. You should be running *to* Me, not running *from* Me. Even if I have to 'get your legs,' I still love you and I will hold you."

Jesus says to us, "The devil will try to wear you out. Run to Me." Jesus can't love us more than He loves us now. And He has never loved us less than He loves us now. His love is eternal and unconditional—*agape*. He loves us despite, not because of.

I Know What I'm Doing

God has His reasons for what He allows. Some of those reasons will not be found in what Jesus experienced because they can't apply to Him.

A man came to our church to share with us on prayer. He was teaching on what we commonly call the *Lord's Prayer.* He told us that really wasn't the *Lord's Prayer.* The *Lord's Prayer* was really John 17. And then he pointed out why the one in Matthew 6 was not it. Jesus didn't inherit the sin nature from Adam. He had no sin to be forgiven.

The late Dr. J. Vernon McGee stated that we are invincible until God is through with us as long as we are in His will. A man walked up to Dr. McGee after he said that and told him he understood the concept.

"If I walk out into the street and get hit by a car, nothing will happen because it's not my time."

"If," Dr. McGee replied, "you walk out into these busy streets and get hit, it *is* your time!" Why? Not God's will.

A Golden Opportunity

We really don't know what we're made of until the test comes. God already knows. We need to know. Peter thought he knew, but each time, he messed up. Later, he was able to pen the following reason God allows us to "go through":

> *That the trial of your faith, being much more precious than of gold that perisheth, though it be tried with fire, might be found unto praise and honour and glory at the appearing of Jesus Christ:*
> ***1 Peter 1:7***

Our faith is tested for the purpose of purification. The idea is the refining of gold. Heat is applied until the gold melts and begins to separate itself from all impurities. The impurities are removed. The gold is just right when the smelter can see his image in the molten gold. What is God doing with *us*? Conforming us to His image and likeness. There's a lot of Ford inside Ford that God cannot use. So, He needs to get Ford out of Ford until He sees Himself. How does God do that? In the crucible of trial and testing. Why?

> *...tribulation worketh patience; and patience, experience; and experience, hope: and hope maketh not ashamed; because the love of God is shed abroad in our hearts by the Holy Ghost which is given unto us.*
> **Romans 5:3-5**

TIMELESS TRUTH

The trouble we're going through is for the future we're on our way to!

We would not be at the level of maturity we are presently had it not been for what we have gone through. We would not have the kind of relationship with Christ we now enjoy had we not gone through some things. We learn more in the valleys than we do on the mountain tops. How much value does your faith have?

There is the story of a man who befriended an entomologist—a person who studies insects. He found a jiggling chrysalis on the ground and felt sorry for the poor butterfly trying to get out, so he decided to help. He cracked the chrysalis slightly to aid the butterfly in its escape. When he returned the next day, the butterfly was dead. He called his friend the entomologist.

"I don't understand it," he lamented. "I opened the chrysalis to help, but it's dead."

Here's what the bug doctor told him: "When you opened the chrysalis, you circumvented the process God designed for that butterfly to be strong and to fly. Using its wings to get out actually brought other dynamics together so that it could fly. So, it died."

Our faith has great value to God and He wants to conform us to His image. God not only wants to divulge the nature of our faith, He wants to strengthen it so we can fly. And, yes, things can get so uncomfortable that we want OUT of the process NOW. But if God allows that, we circumvent the process that purifies and strengthens our faith.

> *Then said the Lord unto Moses, Behold, I will rain bread from heaven for you; and the people shall go out and gather a certain rate every day, that I may prove them, whether they will walk in my law, or no.*
> ***In Exodus 16:4***

God's purpose in dispensing manna to His people the way He did was to test them, not for Himself, but for their own benefit. They needed to know where they were spiritually, especially along the lines of obedience and submission. He would feed an estimated two million people each day for 40 years until they entered the Promised Land. The original plan was that they would make the journey in eleven days. Because of their disobedience, the trip lasted 40 years.

What was the test? "Will you be satisfied with my supply?" They failed the test. They wanted meat. They began complaining. God wanted them to take Him at His Word and be content with His provision in the face of the promise of coming abundance. He gave them what they wanted but "sent leanness into their soul" (Psalm 106:15).

For Your Sanctification
And thou shalt remember all the way which
the Lord thy God led thee these forty years in the
wilderness, to humble thee, and to prove thee, to know
what was in thine heart, whether
thou wouldest keep his commandments, or no.
Deuteronomy 8:2

God would make them a special people set aside just for Himself. He would sanctify their body (dietary laws), soul (civil laws) and spirit (moral laws). They were a people unlike any other. No graven images. No tossing around the name of their God like the heathen nations. Serving an invisible God for Whom the evidence of His existence was the cloud by day, the fire by night, the manna in the morning and an undefeated army.

After all God had done, could the Israelites even begin to trust the God Who had rescued them from slavery and had made them the promise of a land flowing with milk and honey? Each time they hit a glitch, the people complained, blamed Moses, moaned about returning to Egypt (where they'd be enslaved again on the spot) and created a visible god—a golden calf. And, they partied.

The question for us is how much do we trust our God in the midst of temptation and trial? What if there is no miracle to get the house out of foreclosure? What if there is no miraculous healing? What if Junebug doesn't come home this year? What if you have to take the bus after the repo man gets your truck? What will you do? What if you don't find a job before the unemployment runs out? Is our faith in His provision or His Person? Will we be able to honor His unseen plans for us?

> *That through them I may prove Israel, whether they will keep the way of the Lord to walk therein, as their fathers did keep it, or not.*
> **Judges 2:22**

God didn't remove all the heathen inhabitants from the land of promise. He left all the little "rooty-poots" there as "thorns" (v.3) to continue to fine tune His people in obedience and holiness. Now they would have to co-labor with God in obedience and submission to completely come into their promise. Then the rest of the land could be cleared out. Unfortunately, they fell into a cycle of idolatry and rescue. Nations that should have been annihilated would indeed be thorns to them even hundreds of years later.

We want to pass the test. In Genesis 22, the Lord tested Abraham, who was asked to give up his son of promise. There is no recorded argument from Abraham because he is confident that God's Word will not fail—his son will be all that God has said. Abraham passed the test.

God wants us with a faith that will trust and lean more wholly on the Lord Jesus Christ. Yield not to temptation. Jesus is our Source for victory.

3 Listen to Jesus, Your Teacher

LIFE—OUR CLASSROOM

Life is indeed a classroom of learning and tests. Jesus is our Master Teacher by book and example. Problems are the professors. Trials are teachers. Conflict, controversy and consternation are part of the curriculum. Advancement is through adversity. We are permanent students who do not have the option of having the class as an elective or the choice of auditing the class. Class is in session. Pay attention. If you sleep in class, what you miss may determine whether you stand or fall.

TIMELESS TRUTH

HOPE:
"out-stretched neck" –
Joyful anticipation of good based on God's Word.

Jesus is being tested in the classroom of life (Matthew 4:1-11). He's being tested prior to the inception of His earthly ministry. In the realm of biblical numbers, 40 is the number of testing. Jesus spent forty days in the wilderness being tested, not for Himself but for us. He submitted Himself completely to the human condition and experienced everything that we go through so that when we pray in our time of need, in our time of temptation, it would be with confidence that our God, our Lord, our Savior not only completely understands, but is able and willing to flex His muscles as God to intervene on our behalf.

As our Master Teacher, Jesus not only modeled for us how to respond to temptation, but taught us principles and gave us revelation on the very nature of temptation.

1. WE LEARN SUBMISSION TO THE FATHER GOD'S WILL

Jesus taught us to obey the will of the Father through the example of His own obedience. The Bible says that Jesus humbled Himself as a human and like a servant even to the death of the cross (Philippians 2:8). Obedience is simple, but it is not always easy. In the Matthew passage, Jesus faces 40 days of fasting and being in the wilderness with its desert heat and wild animals. He was led there by the Holy Spirit for the purpose of being tested. Although He was fully God and fully man, it was the human that was being tested and tempted and tried. Jesus taught us through this that we too, can have the victory if we rely totally on the Lord in temptations, tests and trials. And, should we fall and become "sanctified suckers" of Satan, God will use that to fine tune us, get us back on track and make us complete in Him.

What God Allows (Job 1–2)

God sometimes allows the enemy of our souls to bring temptation to us. We are the circled about, hedged-in people of God. No one and nothing gets to us unless God allows it. Big Mama died. God allowed it. Job lost. God allowed it. The nuclear reactor incident in Japan. God allowed it. The trouble in the Middle East. God allowed it. Gas prices. God allowed it. We are not like everyone else in the world. We are under the sovereign control of the Sovereign God. Our attitudes should be reflective of the fact that we understand this. So then, even in the middle of temptation and trial, we do not sorrow as those who are hopeless.

In the book of Job, it was God Who initiated the conversation with Satan about Job. Why? Because God knew the outcome of the ordeal that Job would go through. Because as a "perfect and an upright man" as Job was, there were things Job needed to learn about God that only this experience could accomplish. At the end of his trial, Job himself said to God, "I have heard of thee by the hearing of the ear: but now mine eye seeth thee. Wherefore I abhor myself, and repent in dust and ashes" (Job 42:5-6). Job had experienced God. God was no longer a faceless, voiceless, non-relational entity to Whom Job made sacrifices for fear of reprisal.

Jesus is led into the place of temptation by the Holy Spirit. Jesus is God. But in His humanity, He will enter into the experience of His creation. As a man, He will set in motion the redemption of creation lost by not succumbing as Adam and Eve did, to the temptations of the enemy. He will identify with the human condition as He submits obediently to the will of the Father, and He will be victorious. We learn from Jesus to trust and obey in those times when God allows what we do not understand.

The Cod and the Catfish

There is the tale of the cod and the catfish. The story goes that in shipping cod fish from the east coast to the west coast, whether fresh or frozen, they just didn't maintain their meatiness or lovely taste. Someone trying to solve the problem noticed that when catfish—a natural enemy of the cod—was put into the cod's environment, the cod maintained its meatiness and flavor. The east coast began shipping live cod with catfish mixed in and it worked—the cod arrived fresh, meaty and tasteful. There was something about being chased by a catfish!

Could it be that God allows some adversity—temptation—to keep us on our game? To have a testimony of what God can do for others experiencing the same thing? The overriding question is, will we trust God under such circumstances? By allowing and bringing us through these things, God makes us presentable for His glory.

God also allows temptation to divulge the content of our faith, not for Himself, but for us—so that *we* know where we are. So that *we* know what we will do when the heat is turned up. So that *we* can know where we are in our relationship with

God. So that *we* know to what extent we really trust the Lord. So that our faith is strengthened—we are transformed from "faith to faith" (Romans 1:17).

When we are tempted, what is our first reaction? Do we run to God? Do we draw near to God? Does our daily living give any indication of that? If we were to interview elements of our daily living, what would they say? What would our checkbook say? What would our time say? What would our service say? Is our character improved or the lack thereof exposed? Jesus experienced obedience through what He was allowed to suffer (Hebrews 5:7-9). So too, our character is developed through learning obedience.

2. WE LEARN ABOUT THE DEVIL AND HIS STRATEGIES

Let me be clear: the devil is not in hell, nor does he want to be. The devil does not rule hell. He is called the "prince of the power of the air" (Ephesians 2:2). The kingdoms of this world —systems—were turned over to him by Adam and Eve when they sinned in the Garden. But God is still King of kings and Lord of lords. And, the last time I looked, a prince was subject to the King.

The devil is not omniscient (all-knowing), omnipotent (all powerful) nor omnipresent (everywhere at the same time). Were he omniscient, he would have known he couldn't defeat God. Were he omnipotent, God would no longer be God. Were he omnipresent, he couldn't have been expelled out of heaven. He is limited by the sovereignty of God for God's purposes.

About His Strategies

The enemy of our souls works through three strategies: lust of the eyes, lust of the flesh and the pride of life. Whenever temptation comes, the root will always be found in one of these three ways.

Lot is a picture of a worldly Christian tempted in all areas and failed. Lot and Abraham were both wealthy and had lots of livestock. So much so, until their herdsmen were getting into it. They need their own space. Abraham graciously left it up to Lot, who saw beautiful pasture land and took it.

In Genesis 13, Lot chose greener pastures, but moved from those greener pastures into the city of Sodom to do business, while Abraham remained in tents living on the land—ready to pick up and go when God gave the word. This is the first hint of living in a house in Genesis. Lot has set down roots. It's obvious he does not plan to continue on the journey with Abraham.

Lot has determined, "I'm goin' to Pill Hill, put my Beamer and my Mercedes in my two-car garage ... I am here to stay."

By Genesis 18, God has heard the iniquitous cry of Sodom and Gomorrah and after negotiating with Abraham for the souls of Lot's family, is about to destroy those cities.

In Genesis 19, Lot, his wife and two daughters must be escorted out of the city to safety before its destruction since ten righteous people were not found there according to God's agreement with Abraham. Lot's other daughters and sons-in-law had refused to come, and Lot's wife would lose her life for looking back.

Lot wants to stay over in Zoar (little city) rather than listen to the angels and head for the mountains. That doesn't work out for him—it's a scary place. And he winds up in the mountains with his two daughters anyway.

His daughters, reacting to the crisis, decide that they'll never get married and have families, so let's get with dad. There's an entire teaching here about the effect of our choices on our children. Now, where did they get such an idea?

So the daughters broke out the Cristal, got dad inebriated and the result was Moab, meaning "of his father." And, Benammi (progenitor of the Ammonites), which means "son of my people" by Lot's youngest daughter. So these girls have committed incest—inbreeding. These guys will call Lot daddy and granddaddy. That's bad. You think soap operas are hot—you need to read your Bible. Soaps have nothing on the Bible!

Now. Is God still sovereign? How do we know? Deuteronomy 2:23 states that no Moabite can enter into the house of the Lord for ten generations. A generation is 40 years, so we're talking 400 years. Because Lot gave in to the lust of his eyes (the lush land to the east), the lust of the flesh (moved to Sodom to do business despite the lifestyle there) and pride of life (his possessions and position in Sodom), the consequences of his poor choices traveled for generations.

The nations of Moab and Ammon should have never existed and thus, the messes that sprang up through the years would have never occurred. Israel would not have been fighting with Moab and Ammon. Elimelech, Naomi's husband would not have gone to Moab during the famine in Bethlehem and died, his sons may not have died and Naomi would not have suffered so. But then, the salvation of Ruth from whom would come David the king, shows God's ability to take generational mess and turn it into an everlasting message of hope.

Satan showed Jesus the kingdoms under his control that had been delivered to him by Adam and Eve through their wrong choice—just as Lot made wrong choices—and offered them to Jesus in return for worship. It would be easy, just fall down and worship. No cross. No mess. No muss. We learn from Jesus again the importance not only of God's Word, but the application of the principles therein as Jesus' response to the devil is, "Get away from Me, *for it is written*, 'worship the Lord and serve Him only'" (Matthew 4:10). Paradise lost is restored—God's way.

Misuse of God's Word

The devil wanted Jesus to violate God's Word. He wants us to do the same. Bible reading and Bible study are so important! Everything we hear or read from folks is not always correct. Know the Word! Sometimes, I get emails checking me on something I've said. I talk a lot. I say stuff. I'm human. I make mistakes. Absolutely! Check it out!

Jesus uses God's Word to respond to the devil in every instance. At one point, the enemy uses—or, misuses—God's Word to get Jesus to sin. But Jesus uses the Word right back at him—and correctly! Jesus teaches us to know, love and use God's Word as a weapon in defeating temptation.

True story. I travel quite a bit, and right on Jeffery Boulevard there is a viaduct with signs stating that the clearance is 11'8". On a number of occasions, I've seen trucks that attempted to clear that viaduct and literally tore the tops off their vehicles and were stuck there. I thought to myself, *these guys can't be that stupid.*

One day, I got out of my car to investigate this phenomenon. There were three places to pass under that viaduct and all with a stated clearance of 11'8". Guess what I found out? Two underpasses on each side were new and indeed cleared at 11'8". The middle pass was old, lower and had a sign stating the same thing. Therefore, anytime a truck went under the middle pass, there was trouble. The sign needed to be changed by the city!

We are learning from Jesus to be Acts 17:10-11 Christians—like the Bereans. Everybody using a Bible or having a radio or TV program is not properly interpreting the Word of God. The devil will use Scriptures, taking them out of context, adding to them and misquoting them.

Making Consequences Inconsequential

Never once does the devil do the courtesy of mentioning the consequences of giving in to the temptation to Jesus. Neither does he do that with us believers. In fact, with Eve (Genesis 3:4-5), he says they'll be like gods knowing good and evil, which is true. But he doesn't tell her the high price of that knowledge—death. It is a trick of the enemy to not reveal consequences of giving in to temptation or to make us think there are no consequences or... (and this is a juicy one)—that we'll get away with it. NOT HAPPENING.

In Judges 2:22, God shares His reason for not totally wiping out all the nations in the Promised Land. It was to test the faith and obedience of His people. He had broken the backs of the mightiest nations. What was left were the weaker nations that the Israelites should have been able to handle but didn't. Rather than beat them, they joined them. First, they made them servants, when they should have destroyed them. And, secondly, they just didn't want to fight—to go to war.

The consequence was that there was unconquered territory. Pockets of resistance. Always remember, anything you don't conquer *now* will conquer you later. It may seem inconsequential *now*, but later, its influence and power will be overwhelming. It will control you because whatever it is was not dealt with—annihilated.

For instance, Gath went unconquered (Joshua 11:22) and later, the Israelites would deal with Goliath—from Gath. And Ashdod. Later, the Ark of the Covenant would be captured and taken there (1 Samuel 5:1).

They didn't wipe out the Amalekites, and its king, Agag almost got away (1 Samuel 15:9-33). He didn't but somehow his seed did. Several hundred years later, Haman the Agagite attempted to wipe out all the Jews in Persia (Esther 3:6). It is interesting to note that King Saul, a Benjamite was the culprit. A few hundred years later, it would be Esther and Mordecai—Benjamites—who would finish the job their forefather Saul had left undone.

We cannot afford to say, "Oh, it's not a big deal." It will be a big deal later. Take care of it now.

In the wilderness, Jesus doesn't entertain the temptation, He doesn't argue with the tempter and He continually uses the Word of God to check him and finally rebukes him and walks away. Jesus was well aware of the consequences of any disobedience. By His example, Jesus teaches us to do the same.

3. WE LEARN HOW JESUS IS OUR HIGH PRIEST

Jesus is our High Priest (Hebrews 4:14-16) and because He entered the human condition and experience, He is able to sympathize and empathize with us. Because He overcame sin and weakness as a human being, He is able to bring us to victory as our Example and Teacher because He was tempted in all points just like us—but without sin.

We are therefore able to obtain mercy and access the help we need in our time of temptation and trial and tribulation. Because He is also completely God, we have power and authority through His Name and His blood and His Holy Spirit to fulfill the purpose for which He created us.

Jesus is our High Priest, having offered Himself up and become the ultimate and only eternally acceptable Sacrifice for our sins. Through Him, through His blood, we are forever accepted in the Beloved.

4. WE LEARN TO BE EXAMPLES

The first Adam failed, the Second Adam got the victory. The Second Adam—Jesus—is now our Example. He has shown us how to overcome, empowered by the Holy Spirit and the Word of God as our weapon of choice—just as He did in the wilderness.

So we are examples both to other believers and to those who are without Christ. To one - to equip, encourage and enlighten (Ephesians 4:11-16) for the sake of the Body of Christ. To the other, as ambassadors for Christ (2 Corinthians 5:19-21), reconciling those who are without Christ to Him through our very lives. We are living epistles, written of God and read of men, drawing them into His Kingdom.

5. WE LEARN THAT TEMPTATION IS NOT SINGLE-FACETED

Temptation is not limited to a single focus and is multi-faceted by:

Design, Dimension, Desire, Designation

The enemy *designs* temptations to get us to violate God's Word and God's will both written and spoken; both communal and personal. He attacks in both the spiritual, physical and mental *dimensions*. He preys on the *desires* that are already inside us and presents us with the opportunities to fulfill those desires, again, outside the will and Word of God. He has *designated* the lust of the eyes, the lust of the flesh and the pride of life as his foundational places from which the temptation is to be launched.

The first test, for example, was *designed* to get Jesus to violate the will of God by turning stones into bread. Nothing wrong with turning stones into bread. It simply was not the will of God at this time. Later, in feeding 4000 and 5000, bread *and* fish would be miraculously multiplied.

Dimensionally, to have done so would have been a spiritual violation involving physical objects and mentally would have Jesus thinking He didn't have to obey the Father. Game over.

Jesus had just completed a 40-day fast, was famished and *desired* food. The enemy presented Him with an illegitimate opportunity to fulfill that legitimate desire. Jesus refused and opted for God's Word (Luke 4:3-4).

The devil's *designated modus operandi* is always via the lust of the eyes, the lust of the flesh and the pride of life. Jesus' designated the Word of God and the Holy Spirit to be His sources, His foundation, His lifelines.

Jesus teaches us to use the Word of God to answer every challenge presented by the enemy, and to be filled with the Holy Spirit (Ephesians 5:17-19). Paul admonishes Timothy to correctly use the word of truth (2 Timothy 2:15). Why? Because God's Word is alive and powerful and carries authority (Hebrews 4:11-13). When used correctly, in context.

6. We Learn That Everyone is Tempted

Temptation is not sin. How do we know? Because Jesus was tempted. After the victory. After the Father declares from His throne that Jesus is His Beloved Son in Whom He is very pleased. After the Father rips the heavens open. After the Holy Spirit descends on Jesus and fills the Son of Man to overflowing. After the Holy Spirit drives Him into the wilderness. The devil challenged that statement and the confirmations that were given. Jesus met the challenge and was victorious.

Temptation is not selective. The enemy goes after anybody he can. No one is exempt. He is called the "accuser of the brethren" (Revelation 12:9-11). But Jesus overcame and is our "Advocate" (1 John 1:1-3) for those times when we miss the mark.

Temptation is not to be sought. We are never to think that if we do what we know is opposed to the Scripture and known will of God that it will ever be OK or permissible. We are not to purposely put ourselves in the way of temptation. Never put that challenge out there to the enemy, "Take your best shot!" Jesus was *driven* into the wilderness to be tempted (Mark 1:12). It was the will of God in operation. Only God has that authority.

That's Bootleg!

There is a *Redbox* in front of the Walgreens where I go for my wife's meds. There's always a guy standing out there. I figure after a 60-hour work week, I want to kick back with a movie. Whenever I go to the *Redbox*, he catches me.

"Pastor! Don't waste your money on that! Come on over here! I got some good stuff for you with no cussin' in it!"

I decided one day, I had to talk to this guy.

"Man," I said, "you know I'm a pastor, right?"

"Yeah."

"Why is it every time I come up here, you keep trying to get me to buy this bootleg stuff? And I'm gonna be honest with you. Sometimes I *do* want it. Five dollars is cheaper than retail. But I'm not getting it and let me tell you why.

"I'm not gonna get in the pulpit and tell my congregation to have integrity before God and I'm buyin' bootleg videos. Imagine someone comin' to my house and seein' all these bootleg videos. You're stealing."

And then he said this: "I got other pastors who buy 'em off of me!" Oh, no! You see, we have to make these kinds of decisions every day.

When we complain about the attacks of the enemy, remember, he's doing his job. He is here to "kill, steal and destroy" (John 10:10). That's like LeBron James telling the coach, "Stop those guys from trying to block me!" But Jesus has overcome on our behalf and teaches us how to be the overcomers He has crafted us to be—like LeBron James.

TIMELESS TRUTH

ABIDE IN CHRIST —THAT'S WHERE THE VICTORY IS!

Christ on the Cross *Purchased Our Justification,*
Freeing Us From Damnation *of the Devil*
Christ in the Wilderness *Protected Our Sanctification,*
Freeing Us From Domination *of the Devil*
Christ in the Resurrection *Provided Our Glorification,*
Freeing Us From Destination *of the Devil*

4 Listen to Jesus, Your Historian

HISTORICALLY SPEAKING...

There are just three recorded accounts in Scripture where the devil speaks. The first is in Genesis 3, where the serpent talks to Eve. We must assume there was a time when snakes—and animals—could talk. Or, humans were at such a level of intelligence that they could understand the language of animals. But serpents talked and they walked. Part of the curse on the serpent after the fall was that it had to move on its belly, it couldn't get around on foot anymore. After 6000 years, they still slither on their belly. And, some "snakes" still walk. Amen.

The devil talks to Eve about the Word of God. Basically, what we have here is that the first time the devil talked, he talked to humans about God.

The second time the devil speaks is recorded in Job 1-2. He is the accuser of the brethren and God points out His servant Job to which the devil replies, "Job fears You for nothing. Turn him over to me and I'll take care of him for ya." God turns him over with limitations. Now we see the devil talking to God about a human.

In Matthew 4:1–11, the devil is talking to the God-Man. We know he is a liar and a murderer from the beginning. In each event, he lied. When he talked to the humans about God, he lied. When he talked to God about a human, he lied. When he talked to the God-Man, he lied. When he lied to the humans about God, he lied about a place. When he lied to God about the human, he lied about a person. When he lied to the God-Man, he lied about a purpose.

If you are in the right place, if you are the right person and have the right purpose, don't be surprised if the devil lies *on* you or *to* you. That's his job. Sometimes in ministry, we get upset wondering why we're being attacked. It's not always because we're doing something wrong—but because we're doing something right.

The Thrill of Victory—The Agony of Temptation

Both biblical and secular history record the downfall of prominent figures after having achieved great success or having done some great exploit. If we were to interview these figures, in retrospect, they would say that they had no clue of the impending temptation to which they succumbed and that led to their demise or public embarrassment.

Let's take a deeper look at some of those in history who went from victory to vanity. From being victorious to being vanquished.

Noah who'd disciplined himself to obey God, by building an ark that was 120 years in the making along with the sermon of warning he preached: "It's gonna rain." Or, if you prefer proper English: "It's going to rain." God needed to speak to Noah only once. Noah had never seen rain, but God said it and Noah preached it. Why? Because he believed it (Hebrews 11:1).

What great faith to undertake such a project obediently. We can be sure Noah was ridiculed by the people for such a sermon. But there was a silent witness—the ark that had been steadily taking shape for 120 years. The daily clanging and banging that people heard as Noah worked faithfully (James 2:17-18), perhaps in the midst of jokes, sabotage and harassment.

But, then, what happens? Noah comes off the boat, sees some Gray Goose, some Jack Daniels or whatever folks were drinking—and he gets drunk. Right after the victory he gets drunk and things happen (Genesis 9).

King David looking out on a rooftop at a woman bathing instead of being at war. Why? Victory! Vanity! He was the *man*! He'd won wars, killed bears and lions with his bare hands, slain giants, wiped out heathen cities... No one dared put him in check. He was loved, respected and feared. He could do what he wanted and he wanted that woman on the roof.

His giving in to temptation would cost him public embarrassment, several lives and his family would pay for *his* sins for generations. To add insult to injury, David knew who the woman was: the wife of one of his officers, the daughter of one of his fighting men and the granddaughter of one of his counselors.

Solomon was the wisest man who ever lived. And, the wealthiest. Prolific writer, scientist, riddle solver, diplomat. Stuck on stupid! Forgot where all that wisdom came from and at some point, it became the wisdom of this world. Heathen wives and concubines played him big time and he allowed them to introduce ecumenism into the kingdom—everybody has his or her own god. He ended up worshiping theirs and that's how he died. Generations of his descendants paid for his spiritual rebellion.

Each of the above fell in the area of their strength. Noah was disciplined. He became undisciplined. David was a man after God's own heart and filled with integrity. He fell in that area. Solomon's strength was wisdom. He became unwise. So it has been throughout history. Think: Alexander the Great, Napoleon ...

The Thrill of Victory—Period

Jesus' great success is recorded in Matthew 3:13-17. While we commonly recognize the success or victory to be in the announcement of God the Father publicly acknowledging that Jesus is indeed His Son and that He is well pleased with Him, there is an overlooked element of victory here also.

For thirty years Jesus had submitted Himself to the human condition and remained sinless—from infancy through childhood and into adulthood. Now He stood in the Jordan to be drenched with the baptism of repentance, having nothing for which to repent.

But in obedience to His Father and for the sake of His redemptive mission, Jesus submitted Himself to that baptism of repentance. And, from heaven, God gives Him attestation, confirmation, acknowledgment—"This is my beloved Son in Whom I am well pleased" (Matthew 3:17). It is the inception of His Messianic ministry and God puts a sanction on the Lord Jesus Christ and then what happens? He is immediately led into the wilderness by the Holy Spirit to be tempted of the devil.

> *[Jesus] made himself of no reputation, and took upon*
> *him the form of a servant, and was made in the likeness*
> *of men: and being found in fashion as a man, he*
> *humbled himself, and became obedient unto death, even*
> *the death of the cross. Wherefore God also hath*
> *highly exalted him, and given him a name*
> *which is above every name:*
> **Philippians 2:7-9**

In Matthew 4:1-11, that humility is being challenged and the devil hopes to get Jesus to pack up that humility and break out as the heretofore hidden Son of the Most High God, do a few parlor tricks and unwittingly abort the entire mission. Did not happen. Praise God.

HISTORICAL ENEMIES
The World—The External Enemy

We are born into a world of sensory perception: sight, sound, taste, touch, smell. It is literally a leap of faith to live and move and have our being in Christ as Savior, His Word as our guide and the Holy Spirit as our Power Source when we've been in this physical world all our lives. But, it is not impossible. As we abide in Christ and His Word abides in us, our spiritual perception sharpens, faith increases and victory comes (1 John 5:4).

The Flesh—The Internal Enemy

The flesh is that soulish part of us that includes the mind, the emotions and the will. What we think, how we feel and what we want. Not always in line with what God's will is for us. The Bible says, "flee youthful lusts" (2 Timothy 2:22). Get away from the worldly craving for what's new and trendy and curious and forbidden. Many in the past and even now have been led astray that way. Don't bother looking into it, head in the direction of God to avoid being entrapped. Run, Forrest, run!

The Devil—The Infernal Enemy

The devil has always teamed up with the world to cause believers to stumble and fall. The spiritual with the physical. The unseen with the seen. The unfamiliar with the familiar. The Bible tells us to resist the devil (James 4:7). How? By submitting to God. With what God says through His Word and being powered by the Holy Spirit. And since the devil and the world team up, add faith, which is how the world is overcome.

Name That Devil

Historically the enemy has been given names in the Bible describing his nature:

Lion—wants to devour the people of God *(2 Corinthians 11:3)*

Serpent—wants to deceive the people of God *(Genesis 3:1)*

Dragon—wants to destroy the people of God *(Revelation 12:9)*

Wolf—wants to defeat the people of God *(John 10:12)*

Accuser—wants to defame believers *(Revelation 12:10)*

Adversary—wants to depose God's people *(1 Peter 5:8)*

Antichrist—wants to defy the Messiah *(1 John 4:3)*

Enemy—hateful, hostile to God's people *(Matthew 13:38-39)*

God of this world—god of this age *(2 Corinthians 4:3-4)*

Lucifer—morning star *(Isaiah 14:12)*

Father of lies—creator of lies *(John 8:44)*

Prince of the power of the air—atmospheric region *(Ephesians 2:1-2)*

Ruler of this world—worldly systems *(John 12:31)*

Tempter—wants to test and entice God's people *(Matthew 4:3)*

Thief—wants to steal from God's people *(John 10:10)*

The Enemy's Prey

Be sober, be vigilant; because your adversary the devil
walks about like a roaring lion,
seeking whom he may devour.
1 Peter 5:8

Ever watch *Wild Kingdom*? I love that show! My wife wonders how I can stand to watch animals eat each other. Listen, I cheer them on! Maybe it's a guy thing. Or having been in the Marines (*semper fi!*) Any-who, the old lion goes out with the pride—the females—to hunt. Why? Strategy. He's old, usually has lost his teeth and doesn't have the power for the kill that he used to have.

His job is to spot easy prey in the herd: the sick, the weak and the young. He then roars really loud—it's said that a lion's roar can be heard from five miles away. The prey runs in the opposite direction where the females are waiting. And ... they pounce! Once the prey is disabled, the lion comes to feast first. Then the females. Then the cubs.

Like the lion, the devil's strategy is to go after the isolated, the weak, the sick and the newbies of the believers. Peter therefore admonishes us to be watchful and on guard. The elder saints should be guarding and schooling the younger ones so that they are not taken captive and devoured by the enemy. And it is incumbent on us to make it our business to grow in grace and in the knowledge of our Lord and Savior Jesus Christ. The enemy can't steal our souls, so he attempts to steal our testimony. How many generals of the faith have we been inspired by only to discover some shortcoming that put a serious hole in that testimony? We must be on guard.

TIMELESS TRUTH

1 Peter 5:8
Detect Satan's Wiles
Expect Satan's Wiles
Deflect Satan's Wiles

HISTORICAL VICTORY

Victory for God's people has come through the five following ways, and Jesus demonstrated this in His wilderness experience:

> ***Emphasize God as Priority***—Jesus, both in the wilderness and throughout His ministry emphasized that His priority was to do the will of the Father, no matter what.
>
> ***Expose God's Person***—When we honor God, He honors us. When we depend on God, He comes through. Victory is assured.
>
> ***Execute His Plan***—Circumvent *your* purpose for *His* purpose.
>
> ***Exercise His Power***—Be filled with the Holy Spirit.
>
> ***Express His Praise***—Realize that everything is for the glory of God

There are no new methods for walking in victory in the arena of temptation. Everything we need to know is contained in a powerful book called the Bible. God Himself in the Person of Jesus Christ demonstrated that it *is* possible. He was the landmark case. He *is* our victory!

TIMELESS TRUTH

HOLD it! Don't give place to the enemy!
Toehold – Foothold – Chokehold – Stronghold

---

5 Listen to Jesus, Your Counselor

WONDERFUL COUNSELOR!

They are called by many names: counselor, advisor, mentor, spiritual mother, spiritual father, Godmother, Godfather, confident ... Ideally, they are people God has put in our way through whom He dispenses His wisdom, His will, His instructions. They help us get into the lane in which we belong on life's highway and get up to speed.

While they may play a big role in our lives, they are no substitute for our personal relationship with God and spending time in His presence to speak with and hear from Him. If they are truly wise counselors, they will always point us away from themselves and to God. They play Paul to our Timothy and we in turn will do the same for others.

Throughout the Gospels as we travel with Jesus, we also see that His words and actions and motives always point back to the Father:

JESUS' WORDS

> *For I have not spoken of myself; but the Father which sent me, he gave me a commandment, what I should say, and what I should speak. And I know that his commandment is life everlasting: whatsoever I speak therefore, even as the Father said unto me, so I speak.*
> **John 12:49-50**

JESUS' ACTIONS

> *Believest thou not that I am in the Father, and the Father in me? the words that I speak unto you I speak not of myself: but the Father that dwelleth in me, he doeth the works.*
> **John 14:10**

JESUS' MOTIVES

> *I can of mine own self do nothing: as I hear, I judge: and my judgment is just; because I seek not mine own will, but the will of the Father which hath sent me.*
> **John 5:30**

In fact, during His wilderness journey whenever Jesus is tempted by the devil, His response is always from the written Word and the will of the Father—they are His Counselors. The Father spoke and that settled it for Jesus. He made it His business to get away to a solitary place to be with the Father to commune and communicate with Him (Mark 1:35). Because He submitted Himself to the Father—saying what He said, doing what the Father showed Him—wondrous things would happen during the course of His day. His very *raison d'etre,* His focus, was predicated on these words of His:

> *... My meat is to do the will of him that sent me,*
> *and to finish his work.*
> **John 4:34b**

In Christ, we see what happens when a man submits to the whole counsel of God. And, as Christ gave Himself to the whole counsel of the Father, He now is *our* Counselor Who guides us by His example—most notably during the temptation in the wilderness. And most extravagantly, on the cross.

The greatest achievement of good counseling is inspiring a consistently changing mindset that causes growth and transformation that makes us look more and more like our Master Counselor.

Dark Counsel

The Bible says that the devil can manifest as an angel of light (2 Corinthians 11:14). It looks right. It sounds right. It feels right. It has supporting Scripture. But it's *inspired* by darkness. Following Peter's great confession, when Jesus speaks of His impending death, Peter *in good faith* begins to chide Jesus, stating that such a thing would not happen (Matthew 6:22-24).

Jesus was not rebuking Peter. He was rebuking the devil who was expressing himself through Peter's love and concern for Jesus and through Peter's incomplete understanding of Jesus' mission.

The devil talks to you so that he can talk through you. How he talks to us will not always be immediately recognizable. He may commandeer our anger, bitterness, distrust or other negative emotion and speak through that. He may, as he did Peter, speak through our concern or traditional response mechanism.

Right Counsel, Wrong Source

In Acts 16, Luke reports that as Paul and Silas were on their way to prayer in the city of Philippi, a girl followed them around announcing to everyone that they were servants of the Most High God showing the way of salvation. Nothing wrong with that. After several days of this, Paul was "grieved" with what she was doing. Why? It turns out the young lady was possessed with a spirit of divination which brought her masters lots of money.

But, it was true, wasn't it? Paul and Silas *were* servants of God. They *were* preaching the Gospel. What was the issue? When Paul and Silas moved on (and they would), this young lady would still be in the city doing what she did. If so, several unfortunate things would happen: her credibility would be greater by association with Paul and Silas; new believers would assume she and divination were legitimate; true Christianity would be contaminated by the occult, opening the door for false doctrine; and, all the while, her masters would get richer and she would never be free of that evil spirit.

What does Paul do? Casts the devil out of her. That did not sit well with her masters and Paul and Silas were beaten and hauled off to jail where they sang hymns till the earth quaked and the jail doors opened and the jailer got saved.

True story. Fifteen years ago, our church was working on building and opening a community life center. We were inundated with kids—200 on the waiting list—thanks to Reverend and Mrs. Liles whom we referred to as the Pied Pipers of the Gospel. But we didn't have much money. Down the street was a program with plenty of money, but few kids.

We were approached by a "beverage" company that wanted to help sponsor the center. They would pay three quarters of the cost and the church would pay the other 25%. They wanted the church to have a "vested interest." The catch? They wanted their name on the marquee. No go. What would that say about God's ability to sustain us? What other compromises would come down the road? Jesus, our Counselor will never advise us to meet a legitimate need through illegitimate means.

Believers are just as challenged by the enemy in other areas. Ladies, be careful—the enemy will send Ishmael before God sends Isaac.

Not only is an intimate, working knowledge of God's Word crucial, but an intimate working relationship with God Whose Holy Spirit fills us, speaks to us, empowers us and helps us to "rightly divide the word of truth" (2 Timothy 2:15). Thus, we walk in the light and it enables us to recognize and dispel darkness.

On the other hand, the enemy blinds the minds of those who don't believe (2 Corinthians 4:4) to keep them from the Gospel of light and tries to cloud the minds of believers to make them of none effect (2 Corinthians 10:3-6) through vain imaginations, exalted thinking against God and strongholds. Dark counsel. The devil wants to influence our minds.

Counseling Process

I was reading about a plant called the *sisal* plant. It captured my attention because it flourishes in arid places. One of the foremost exporters of the plant is Mexico. The plant has become valuable because it contains a fiber good for making rope and other products. It's used in marine activities because it handles saltwater well.

Well, someone got a "great idea." They transplanted it here in America in fertile soil in a controlled environment. Sure enough, it grew bigger. However, when it was processed into rope, it crumbled. Why? Here's what they discovered and reported: because the sisal was taken from its natural environment and grown in a controlled environment under what was thought to be better conditions, elements in the natural process were circumvented or altered and it affected the natural abilities of the plant to produce the right fiber content.

I thought to myself, *that's a believer.* The struggle to get what it needed from the arid climate was eliminated and produced a weaker—although bigger—plant. Dealing with the extreme heat was part of the process that led to strong rope from the plant. It *looked* bigger, it *looked* better, but when put to the test—it crumbled.

So, it was the original process that produced the needed strength. It is God's original plan –His will carried out—that makes us the people He wants us to be. Many of us believers are like tea bags—the hotter the water the stronger and more flavorful the tea. As stated in James 1:2-4:

> *My brethren, count it all joy when ye fall into divers temptations; Knowing this, that the trying of your faith worketh patience. But let patience have her perfect work, that ye may be perfect and entire, wanting nothing.*

The struggles we endure now are for the future that we're on our way to. God uses our struggles to develop us. It is God's divine design at work in the middle of our problems, struggles and temptations.

Jesus was aware that there was an ultimate goal in what He was going through in the wilderness. He had to get past what was in His immediate line of vision—the devil and the temptations—for the ultimate vision the Father had shown Him—the salvation of the world. And now, Jesus counsels us to the same goal and focus:

> *Wherefore seeing we also are compassed about with so great a cloud of witnesses, let us lay aside every weight, and the sin which doth so easily beset us, and let us run with patience the race that is set before us looking unto Jesus the Author and Finisher of our faith; who for the joy that was set before him endured the cross, despising the shame, and is set down at the right hand of the throne of God. For consider him that endured such contradiction of sinners against himself, lest ye be wearied and faint in your minds.*
> **Hebrews 12:1-3**

TIMELESS TRUTH

The believer who cannot see the ultimate
Will become slave to the immediate.

Jesus is the Author and Finisher of our faith, our divine Counselor, Who counsels us and walks us through that period between the authorization and completion of our faith for the area in which we are being tempted, tested and tried.

When we do not, will not or cannot see the ultimate goal of God in the midst of those difficult times, we become slaves to the immediate—what we see in front of us. We worry excessively about what's happening, how we'll get through and we harbor fear concerning the outcome.

Case Study

In Luke 22:24-34, Jesus counsels the disciples concerning what it really means to be great. He tells them of things to come: they have a kingdom, they will sit and eat and drink with Jesus in His kingdom and they will judge the twelve tribes of Israel. Wow!

And then, Jesus immediately turns to Peter to share some news with him—the devil wants God to release Peter to him. Why? To "sift" him like wheat—to shake his faith up for the purpose of destroying that faith.

Now, that would actually happen although Peter in "good faith" assures Jesus that he will stand with Him no matter what, not realizing he would deny even knowing Jesus within hours of his declaration. Jesus tells Peter He has prayed for him so that the faith the devil wants to destroy does not fail. In other words, this *will* take place, but the ultimate purpose of God will be served: while Peter's faith will falter, it will *not* fail—he will be strengthened and converted.

He will also ultimately help his fellow disciples who will take a hit in their faith in the next few hours. Peter is the point man the enemy wants to take out. He has been given revelation, walked on water and been made privy to what the majority of the disciples will be unaware of until after Jesus' resurrection. If the enemy takes Peter down, the others will follow.

It does not appear that any of what Jesus said concerning God's ultimate purpose is coming to pass until the day of Pentecost when the Holy Spirit arrives (Acts 2) and Peter preaches the Gospel.

For example, in John 21, even after Jesus' resurrection and appearance, Peter is found not only going back to his former career as a fisherman, but influencing others to do the same. Jesus, however, appears on the shore and puts a stop to that.

Like a good counselor, Jesus gets to the heart of Peter's real issues through pointed questions that Peter must honestly answer, face the truth and get on the road to his conversion and his future, which is also revealed to him by Jesus.

As pronounced as his perceived failures had been, the fulfillment of God's ultimate purpose for his life would be even greater—the salvation of countless thousands all over the known world, the establishment of churches, the training and raising up of other servant leaders and his now fearless defense of the Gospel.

Comprehensive Counseling

The mainstay of counseling is communication. With our God this is done through prayer. We talk with God—we talk to Him and He talks with us. Because Jesus has experienced the human condition victoriously, we have every confidence in whatever He tells us ... He is our Example and Advocate. His counseling is comprehensive, covering every aspect of our lives. He gave us the disciples' prayer in Matthew 6:9-13, as the layout for communication and response:

In verse 11—*give us our daily bread*—we see Jesus' foundational care for life's everyday physical needs. A good counselor recognizes that when people go lacking in the most basic needs it can alter emotional stability and reasoning and the ability to mature properly. It's hard to hear and follow your Counselor's wisdom above a growling stomach or gnawing pain (Mark 8:1-3).

In verse 12—*forgive us our trespasses*—most people wind up in counseling because of issues with another person. It has been shown that when forgiveness ensues, healing and peace usually follow (Matthew 6:14-15). The ability to trust and love in the present is restored and the emotional trauma of the past is cured. Healthy emotions take its place.

In verse 13—*deliver us from the evil one*—our Counselor helps us overcome the fear of the future, assuring His presence and help should trouble arise. We are assured that we are not alone in what we face—everyone is faced with these temptations and trials at some time. Our Counselor assures us He is faithful and that there are limitations on temptations. We will be all good as long as we follow His escape plan (2 Corinthians 10:13).

As with any effective counselor, we will be placed in situations to test our increasing ability to handle issues we may not have handled well before. In Matthew 4:1-11, Jesus sets the example and not only becomes the model for handling such situations, but our Counselor (Hebrews 2:18) because of His successful experience. If we, however, refuse to follow His counsel, when things do not work out, we cannot blame Him. His intent is that we fulfill our purpose and be blessed in our doing.

One more story. A son tells his dad he wants a sports car as his graduation gift. The dad says nothing. On graduation day, Dad gives his son a Bible as a gift. Disappointed, the son walks away, leaving the Bible and heads off to college. Years later, Dad dies and his son is settling his affairs. The son sees the Bible he rejected and guiltily thumbs through it. In it, he finds the paid receipt for the sports car he'd asked of his dad as a graduation gift. The gift was in the Bible he'd rejected. Let it not be so with us. Let us heed our Counselor.

Finally, we have a Wonderful Counselor with an Eternal Life Insurance Plan. It guarantees that the day *will* come when having walked in His counsel will bring an ultimate pay-off of being temptation-free, trial-free and tribulation-free—forever!

6 Listen to Jesus, Your Lord

IS JESUS LORD OF ALL?

Unlike many believers, the devil is always on his job. He never takes a day off. He's on his job every day, seven days a week, 365 days a year, 24 hours a day. He never takes a vacation. He is totally committed to our total destruction. He's always ready to fight us. If he doesn't fight you, perhaps it's because he's already got you.

It gets worse. Not only does he fight us all the time, *we* can't defeat him. He beat Adam and Eve in a perfect world. What makes us think we can whip him in a perverted world? In the Garden, there was no sin, no suffering, no sorrow. There was no crack, adultery, fornication, porn and on and on ... And, he still whipped them.

And so what happened? God had told them that in the day they ate the fruit they would die (Genesis 2:16-17). Some may say, "But they didn't die right away." Well, let's see. They died in their spirits *immediately*. They began to die in their soul *progressively*. They died in their bodies *ultimately*. That's the way death deals with us.

Although we cannot personally defeat him, the Bible says in 1 John 4:4: *You are of God little children and have overcome them because greater is he that is in us than he that is in the world.* He is already a defeated foe because of our Lord and Savior Jesus Christ (Hebrews 2:14). He did it for you and for me.

Do you have big brothers or big sisters? You know, there was a guy named Tony in my neighborhood when I was growing up. A big mouth, little guy with big brothers. He was the baby of nine boys! He was my age, which meant all his brothers were older than I was. He would tell folks, "Get outta my way!" Sure! Go right ahead! You know, we all thought the same thing: *Boy, if your brothers ever die...*

You and I have an elder brother. Whenever we have to deal with the devil, he has to move out of the way. We just run and tell our big brother all about our troubles.

This is where the Lord fulfills the prophecy of Genesis 3:15 in crushing the devil's head and giving us the victory. It begins with the promise in Genesis, continues at Calvary and is consummated at the resurrection. Jesus took care of everything—our justification (Calvary), our sanctification (His Holy Spirit) and our glorification (the resurrection).

So, in justification Christ has done away with the devil's ability to bring us into damnation by His victory on Calvary. In sanctification, Christ has freed us from the domination of the devil through His Holy Spirit Who empowers us as Jesus was empowered in the wilderness. And, in glorification through His resurrection Christ has freed us from the destination of the devil.

So, then, all things are under His feet. Can you see the picture? At Calvary Christ's "heel" was bruised, but in the resurrection, the devil's head was crushed. Our victory does not come from anything we imagine we can do against the devil, but from what Christ has already done. What does Paul say in his closing to the Roman believers?

> *And the God of peace will crush Satan*
> *under your feet shortly.*
> **Romans 16:20**

Under whose feet is the devil? Jesus' feet! Now under whose feet does Paul refer? Ours! Why? Jesus! He's already under Jesus' feet and now Jesus has given us His victory. Jesus is seated at the right hand of His Father far above all principalities and powers. And ... we are seated in Christ. Where? Far above all principalities and powers (Ephesians 2). Whatever is under Jesus' feet is under our feet too. So, we are "more than conquerors" through Jesus Who loves us so (Romans 8:37).

What Shall I Render, Lord?

My granddaughter asked me to buy her some sherbet. "I'll pay you back later," she promised. That was cute. How was she going to pay *me* back? I don't think she even meant it.

I said to her, "What if I get you the sherbet, but the way you pay me back is if I need something done later, I can say, 'Naomi, I need you to do this –'?"

"That's easy," she said.

"What do you mean?"

"I'll just tell you to ask JJ."

How can we repay Jesus for what He did for us on Calvary? We can't. We simply do the things He asks us to do and even then, like my granddaughter who knew she couldn't repay me and would depend on her brother JJ, we have to depend on the Holy Spirit even for the ability to do that.

Oh, Lord, Why Me?

Why does God allow us to be challenged by the devil in the first place? For what purpose does God use testing, trial and temptation?

1. To *divulge* the content of our faith
2. To *determine* our allegiance
3. To *dive* into our character
4. To *direct* our life
5. To *detect* the quality of our life
6. To *depict* our destiny
7. To *disclose* God's plan for us
8. To *discover* our dependency on God
9. To *deaden* our flesh
10. To *demonstrate* God's glory

I Pledge Allegiance to the Lamb!

God does not allow testing, temptation or tribulation so that *He* can find out anything. It is for us to know by experience what we believe, how we will respond or react and where our true allegiance is: to God or self.

Peter meant well, but he wore peppermint socks—his foot was always in his mouth! He let his mouth write checks that his commitment couldn't cash. He swore he'd never abandon Jesus, but he did. At prayer time in Gethsemane, he slept. When Jesus was arrested, he cut off a guard's ear, and in anger, denied knowing Jesus three times. He spoke too soon, boasted too much, prayed too little and acted too quickly.

But, in John 20, Peter comes face-to-face with himself as the resurrected Jesus—in a simple, loving way—gently leads him "back home." Peter, after Jesus' ascension in Acts 2, becomes a prolific dispenser and demonstrator of the Gospel. He is still human, but he is never the same.

What is it the devil wants to do in our lives? What's he going after? The three things that affect everything in our relationship with the Lord Jesus Christ, and that's what he wants to kill, steal and destroy:

> ***The Lordship of Jesus*** *(Luke 6:46)*
> ***The Fellowship with Jesus*** *(John 15:15)*
> ***The Worship of Jesus*** *(John 4:23-24)*

The top question every believer must answer is: Where Christ is with us? What is His position in our lives? If Jesus is not Lord of *all*, then He is not Lord *at* all.

What if God's plan is *Meals on Wheels* or as in the case of Elijah, *Meals on Wings*? Can we wait on the Lord and trust His plan? When I was young, because I was the oldest, I went with my mom to the welfare office and stood in line for her while she sat and waited. I was so embarrassed to be in that line waiting... The government cheese line. Powdered milk. Butter. Powdered eggs. But, listen, that was some delicious cheese. I actually saved one of the boxes to use in a sermon illustration one of these days!

But, the question on the table is, can we let God do things *His* way? The enemy of our souls wants us to compromise God's purpose for our lives. To Jesus, he said, "Turn those stones to bread. Jump off that pinnacle. Just give *me* a couple bars of a good worship tune. Nothing major. What could it hurt?"

To us, he says, "Hey, I know God wants you to go to the mission field, but you've got to live in this world. You've got a great mind. A great education. Make that money!" He wants us to compromise by disobeying the will of God and distorting the word God has spoken to us.

In not trusting Jesus' Lordship in our lives, we limit His ministry in our lives. It doesn't stop it, but it limits it. Remember, the more committed we are to Jesus, the more committed He is to us. What are we to do? How do we submit to the Lordship of Christ? I give all that I am to all that He is:

*Love Jesus **SUPREMELY***
*Trust Jesus **COMPLETELY***
*Obey Jesus **TOTALLY.***

WHAT TO DO WHEN THE DEVIL TALKS TO YOU

Serve Jesus **UNRESERVEDLY.**
Worship Jesus **EXCLUSIVELY.**

Who's in Charge Here?

I paid a visit to my doctor a while back.

"How are you, Rev. Ford?" she greeted me.

"I'm fine, Doc," I answered.

"Yeah. I know you're here because I said I wouldn't give you another prescription without a visit. I don't dispense medication unless I see you. You missed four appointments last year. I saw you in January and it's May—over a year later. I gave you four appointments, but that's okay. Go ahead and die if you want to." Then I got on the scale.

"Oh, let's see...290. Last time you were here last January, you were 292. Oh, whoop-dee-doo! Two whole pounds!"

What could I say? I just sat there and took it.

"So," she continued, "have you been keeping a record of your glucose levels?" Silence. "Do you have a good insurance policy for your wife?"

"Yes, I do," I replied.

"Oh, that's good," she retorted, "you're probably going to need it. Do you have your blood pressure medication? Your pressure is high."

"Oh, yeah," I said. "I didn't take it because I was coming here to see you."

"You don't stop taking your blood pressure medicine because you're coming to see me," she said.

Long story short: I got home and asked my wife, "Do you see anything back here?" I asked as I turned my back to my wife. "Because she chewed me *out!*"

My doctor told me that if I didn't do as instructed, "Find another doctor! I will not be responsible for your death."

You know what she was saying to me? "You are limiting my ability to help you!" That's exactly what we do to Jesus—we limit His *Lordship*—His ability to do what He wants and needs to do in our lives. We limit His might—His power—in our lives. The intensity of His power in our lives comes through *fellowship*—communion. We limit the majesty of Christ in our lives by demeaning the worship of God and His praise when we fail to celebrate God in our lives by our obedience.

Who's on the Throne?

When I am on the altar, Christ is on the throne. In Romans Paul gives us the total package of this *Magna Carta* of the Christian faith:

Romans 1: *All are Guilty*
Romans 2: *Hebrews Guilty with the Law*
Romans 3: *World Guilty without the Law*
Romans 4: *Justification in Christ*
Romans 5: *Justified by Faith in Christ*
Romans 6: *We are Dead to Sin, Alive in Christ*
Romans 7: *Sin Wars*
Romans 8: *Sonship Through the Spirit of Christ*
Romans 9: *Israel's Rejection of Redemption*
Romans 10: *Israel's Need of Redemption*
Romans 11: *Israel's Coming Redemption*

Romans 12: *A Living Sacrifice*
Romans 13: *Obedience in Christ*
Romans 14: *The Law of Liberty and Love*
Romans 15: *Support in Christ*
Romans 16: *Unity in Christ*

And so, we see that Jesus is indeed Lord of all whether we actually give Him His due or not. Our belief or unbelief neither increases nor diminishes Who He is, or His finished work of grace.

Top Dog!

I was given a very expensive dog once. I would have never *bought* him. I named him Boaz. One day, I was reaching into Boaz's cage to get his bowl to feed him. Now, my wife had been saying we needed to get rid of the dog because he'd been growling at folks lately—her, my mother-in-law... I thought, *no. Besides, he wasn't an even-tempered dog anyway.*

But listen, that joker growled at *me*. He snapped at my hand! My wife had to stop me! I was about to kill that dog! You're eating my food, living under the shelter of my roof, I have to pay to have your hair done ... and you're growling at me? He had to go to the pound!

Some of us have teens. We clothe them, feed them, pay the Internet and cell phone bill. Do we let them growl at us? What might Jesus say when we do the same to Him?

You call Me Master and obey Me not
You call Me Light and see Me not
You call Me the Way and walk Me not

Listen to Jesus, Your Lord

You call Me Life and desire Me not
You call Me Wise and follow Me not
You call Me Rich and ask Me not

You call Me Eternal and seek Me not
You call Me Gracious and serve Me not
You call Me Noble and honor Me not
You call Me God and worship Me not
If I condemn you—blame Me not.

Do we have a "time share" relationship with Jesus? He's married to us, but we're "dating" Him. He wants an everyday relationship. But, we sing more lies than we'll ever tell. We sing "Sweet Hour of Prayer" but rarely pray. We sing "We're Marching to Zion" but don't walk into Sunday school. We sing "Amazing Grace" and then doubt our so great a salvation. We sing "O, for a thousand tongues to sing my great Redeemer's praise!" Why would you need 999 more tongues when you're not using the one you have to tell others about Jesus?

How about "Onward, Christian Soldiers" and you've been AWOL all this time? Perhaps these are the real tunes:

Sitting on The Premises
Three Seconds of Prayer
I Love to Tell the Gossip
I Surrender Some
On the Battlefield for My Agenda

Jesus sets the example for Lordship throughout the Gospels, but especially in Matthew 4:1-11. He submits to His Father and

107

we follow suit in submitting to Him. When the devil comes with temptations, who will we serve? Who will we obey?

You know, the first indicators of Jesus not being Lord isn't what we may think—drugs, alcohol, adultery, etc. It will be these: are we in God's Word each day? Are we in communication and communion with God each day?

These things are not the end in themselves, they are the means to entering into that wonderful relationship we want with Him. To knowing Him and loving Him more fully. And, when we do wrong, we feel it more *because* we are coming into a fuller relationship and loving Him more.

After discovering the extent to which my doctor was concerned and cared about me, I made up my mind I was going to do right. I was also confronted with her authority over me. She had the power and the right to withhold any further prescriptions or treatments if I failed to cooperate with what was best for me in her professional opinion.

In fact, she could cut me off as her patient. Her goal was that I live longer, healthier and happier. Does that sound familiar? Choose this day, whom you will serve. Jesus is Lord, no matter what. But—is He YOUR Lord?

7 Listen to Jesus, Your Strategist

The Desert Fox

Erwin Johannes Eugen Rommel (1891–1944), known as "The Desert Fox," was a high ranking, well-respected general in Hitler's military. In World War II, Germany was all over Europe and Northern Africa. Allied powers—which included America—had stayed back, not believing that Hitler would actually do all he'd threatened to do. But when Germans headed toward England, America sat up, knowing she would be next on the agenda.

In Africa, Germany had what was known as the Afrika Corp. Despite the fact that the Allied Forces were superior in number of machines, weaponry and troops, the Germans were wearing the Allied Forces out. It was due to one man's ingenious tactics—Rommel. Rommel was so adept at moving machinery—tanks—and initiating surprise attacks across the desert and taking out enemy troops, he was nicknamed

The Desert Fox. His defeat came at the counter-genius of General Bernard Law Montgomery, known as "The Spartan General."

Montgomery was never interested in the numbers and strengths and abilities of the Afrika Corps. He was only interested in the man behind it: Rommel. If he knew the man, he reasoned, he would be victorious in war. He was successful because he knew Rommel and his tactics.

Our Captain of the Host

We have a superior Person, the Lord Jesus Christ. We have superior precepts and strategies—the Word of God. We have superior forces—all the host of heaven. We have superior troops—the people of God. We have superior power—the Holy Spirit. Then why does our foe have us on the defensive? We have become ignorant of his devices (2 Corinthians 2:11). We don't understand all that we have and we don't know how he works. What we *don't* know can hurt us.

Throughout this book, we have gone over the three main weapons in his arsenal: lust of the flesh, lust of the eyes and the pride of life. His favorite target is the Word of God. That is evident in the very first temptation (Genesis 3) when he attacked the revelation of God's Word to man. He wanted them to:

Doubt God's Word (v.1)
Distort God's Word (vv.2-3)
Deny God's Word (vv.4-5)
Disobey God's Word (v.6)
Destroy God's Word (vv.9-13)

What did the devil do and still does today? Attacked the credibility of God's Word in the lives of His people. Throughout history it has remained his number one tactic.

TIMELESS TRUTH

*The Bible has survived the fires of its foes
And the fanaticism of its friends*

The Test of Time

Let's look at the seventeenth century philosopher Voltaire. He was a deist. He believed in a higher power but refused to acknowledge the only Power—Jesus Christ. His disdain for religion was across the board—he was an equal opportunity hater. As he lay dying, a priest tried to get him to renounce Satan to which Voltaire allegedly said, "Now is not the time to make new enemies." He has unfortunately, learned who the real enemy is.

The devil hates God's Word so much that in 1967, Anton LeVay began the Church of Satan and wrote the Satanic Bible. These are the tenets on which it is based—that Satan represents the following:

1. Indulgence instead of abstinence
2. Vital existence instead of spiritual pipedreams—there is no life after death
3. Undefiled wisdom instead of hypocritical self-deceit—don't love God, love self

4. Kindness to those who deserve it instead of love wasted on ingrates—only Satan deserves it

5. Vengeance instead of turning the other cheek

6. Responsibility to the responsible instead of concern for psychic vampires

7. Man is just another animal like a dog. If you kill him it doesn't matter—there is no life after death

8. So-called sin; if it's evil, he's for it. Don't fight who you are

9. The best friend the church has ever had; he has kept it in business all this time

Still, the best-selling book of all time is the Bible—the Word of God. It should be as well-read as other best sellers.

> *The grass withers, the flower fades, but the word of our God stands forever."*
> **Isaiah 40:8**

Jesus' Strategy

Jesus used the Word—"It is written." We resist the enemy by using the Word of God. Jesus answered the devil in each temptation by quoting Scripture (Matthew 4:1-11). And why not? Jesus is the *Living Word*. Why didn't Jesus just tell the devil to get behind Him, period? Why didn't Jesus say, "*I* say to you"? Let's go the Sermon on the Mount in Matthew 5.

Several times, Jesus begins:

> *Ye have heard that it was said by them of old time*
> **Matthew 5: 21, 27, 28, 31-32, 33-34, 38-39, 43-44**

And Jesus expands:

> *But I say unto you...*
> **Matthew 5: 21, 27, 28, 31-32, 33-34, 38-39, 43-44**
>
> *Jesus is the authority. He is the Word made flesh. But during the temptation, Jesus simply says:*
> *It is written...*
> **Matthew 4: 4, 7, 10**

Jesus uses the written Word. Why? Because *we* can't say, "I say to you!" Jesus is setting the example for us to follow as believers. He is modeling what our response should be. Jesus is telling me that when I am being tempted, I don't use my own perceived authority, I use the authority of the written Word of God! That's powerful. The *Living Word* used the written Word to defeat the enemy. He didn't say, "In My opinion," or "I think," or "It might be true." He didn't quote Oprah or Dr. Phil. He quoted the Word of God.

Voicing Strategy

We know that Matthew's audience was the Jews and Luke's audience was the Greeks—Gentiles. In the wilderness passage the voice each uses is geared to its audience. Matthew uses the "middle voice." He says, "It is written and stands written." It's credible. Put your foot on it. Luke writes in the passive voice. Luke says, "It is written and it is complete." The end. These voices are not exclusive of each other. Put them together and the message is: "It is written, true, credible and complete as it stands."

To those who declare the Bible to be out-of-date, Jesus quoted frequently from the book of Deuteronomy. The testimony is that the Bible is still the best-selling book in the world today, it still changes lives and changes destinies. Some say that folks don't talk King James style. True. So, get a New King James.

Let's Talk a Little Computer History:
- 1975, Apple Computer gets it start in Steven Jobs' garage
- 1975, Bill Gates kicks off Microsoft
- IBM 5100 first personal computer
- 1978, Apple designs inexpensive floppy disk
- Word star introduces word processing
- 1981, Osborne One is first portable computer
- 1983, Word Perfect and Microsoft Word introduced
- 1989, Word for Windows introduced
- 1991, Memory Card introduced
- 1992, Plasma display monitor introduced
- 1993, PDAs introduced
- 1994, Laptops with CD-ROM drives introduced
- 2000, Flash drives introduced
- 2009, IPad introduced

Geez. Look at that! I'd just gotten a Blackberry! I didn't know what to do with it. I was just learning to use the Blackberry. I got a call saying I could upgrade and now I have a Droid. The things I could do on the Blackberry, I don't know how to do on the Droid. And then, someone told me my Droid was outdated. I wanted to know why.

"It's only 3G," they told me.

"3G? What's that?" I asked.

How about medical books? Almost before they're published, they're obsolete with all the new information coming in. BUT...

> *The grass withers, the flower fades,*
> *But the word of our God stands forever."*
> **Isaiah 40:8**

We can keep saying, "It is written," because the Bible is never outdated. Matthew says it can be trusted and it's credible. Luke says it's totally truthful and complete. The Bible is as credible today as it was back then. It's as complete today as it was back then. And Jesus used the Word of God in that wilderness temptation experience on our behalf.

Now, why did Jesus quote Deuteronomy? Deuteronomy is called the Second Law. It was not the second giving of the Law, but the reiteration of the Law. It was given to the generation that succeeded the generation that died in the wilderness. Why did the first generation die in the wilderness?

> *But with whom was he grieved forty years? was it not*
> *with them that had sinned, whose carcasses fell in the*
> *wilderness? And to whom sware he that they should not*
> *enter into his rest, but to them that believed not? So*
> *we see that they could not enter in because of unbelief.*
> **Hebrews 3:17–19**

Jesus is using Deuteronomy because of the generation that failed in the wilderness. But Jesus is the second Adam and He does not fail. The first Adam failed in the Garden. He allowed God's Word to be distorted and doubted it. But the Second Adam stood on it.

I preached a young member's funeral and there were gang members in attendance. Out of eighteen professions of faith, one came back afterward. He was seriously after me. He wanted materials given to him NOW—not mailed later. He knew where he was and he felt the urgency to get into God right away. I went into the back room and got him what he needed and put it in his hands.

"You gonna be here Sunday?"

"Yeah," I told him.

"I'm coming back here Sunday," he said. "I've been in darkness." And you know what? He did! That's the response God wants us to have to His Word. Believe it, grab hold and live it. It's not enough to be a part of a Bible-believing church. We must make sure we're in a Bible-behaving church!

The Right Strategy

In the sport of fencing, a parry is a fitting response with your blade to fend off or block the attack of your opponent. When we respond to enemy attacks with the Word of God, the Word we use must be appropriate to counter the attack. We must:

1. *Read* God's Word—Revelation 1:3
2. *Hear* God's Word—Romans 10:17
3. *Memorize* God's Word—Psalm 119:9, 11
4. *Meditate* on God's Word—Psalm 1
5. *Study* God's Word—2 Timothy 2:15
6. *Obey* God's Word—James 1:22-23

7. *Share* God's Word—Romans 1:15
8. *Believe* God's Word—Hebrews 4:15

9. **Tell** God's Word Like it is—Proverbs 30:5–6

Why Undermine God's Word?

What is the purpose of the enemy undermining God's Word in our lives? We have to know that there's something wonderful and powerful about God's Word. Here's what the enemy's design is:

1. **Discontentment** with God's provision
2. **Desire** things more than God
3. **Declare** your independence from God
4. **Depend** upon human reasoning
5. **Decide** with limited information
6. **Develop** your way to live outside of God
7. **Destiny** fulfilled apart from God's plan for your life

We will find strength from the Lord and His Word by remembering these things.

God Replenishes Us

When the temptations were ended for that time, God the Father sent angels to refresh, replenish and strengthen Jesus. He does the same for us. Angels are assigned to minister for those who belong to Christ (Hebrews 1:14).

An **angel** announced the impending birth to Mary
Angels heralded the birth of Jesus
An **angel** warned Joseph of Herod's murder plot
Angels ministered to Jesus after the temptation

Angels ministered in Gethsemane
Angels observed the crucifixion

Angels were at the post-resurrection tomb
Angels were present after Jesus ascension
Angels will be present for Jesus second coming

Hook!

Hook was hard to lead to Christ. He lived with two women, and he didn't want to hear about Jesus and the Bible. Yet, he was the nicest man you ever wanted to meet. But God had things in hand. Hook called me at 2 am one morning.

"Man, we need Jesus!" Hook was crying and the two women were crying. So I got into my "Gospel buggy"—a car that was given to me when I needed one. Anyway, I'm rolling into Wilkinsburg and the car stops. That's not good. This was my old stomping ground when I was unsaved and selling drugs and robbing people. All I knew to do was pray.

"Lord, protect me because I'm going to do Your will. I got up this early in the morning out of my bed to do Your will. You gotta protect me." And then I see a familiar M.O. I'm walking to Hook's house which is located on a dead-end street and near a cemetery.

A guy steps out in front of me and one behind. I knew what was going on. My brother-in-law and I had pulled that scenario often back in the day. I didn't have any money. What was I going to do? I didn't have a gun since I'd gotten saved.

"Lord, You mean to tell me You're going to let something happen to me before I get to this house?" Suddenly, a squad car came out of nowhere. Just as suddenly, the two would-be perpetrators were gone! I waved at the officers.

"How're you doing, officers?" And I put both hands up—"Thank You, Jesus!" I shouted. The car pulled up and the officer rolled his window down.

"Sir, are you okay?"

"Oh, yes, sir! I'm on my way to lead somebody to Christ!" The officers pulled off.

I get to Hook's house, which is a duplex. But ... there's no name on either bell. Well, he lives on the first floor, so I rang the bottom bell. Makes sense, right? Suddenly, I hear a voice.

"Move back!" So, I moved back. When I stepped back, the angry woman upstairs opened her window and the window pane fell out and landed right where I would have been standing had not that voice told me to move back! She was cussin' up a storm, but my hands were up praising God for not having been accosted by that big windowpane.

"What are you doing out here?" she yelled.

"I'm sorry, Ma'am, but I'm looking for Hook."

"Hook lives downstairs!" and with that she slammed down the frame of the window where the pane used to be.

But the good news is that I led Hook and one of his ladies to the Lord. I wrote in my journal: "I didn't know guardian angels were real. Somebody was watching out for me."

God has us covered. Angels are working on our behalf as we do His will. The victory we experience is for that time. Each victory will help us to win the next victory. Jesus has taught us what to do when the devil talks to you. And, Jesus has covered victory for us—for always.

8 Listen to Jesus, Your Closer

It Ain't Over Until...

There was a highly rated television series on TNT that ran several seasons entitled *The Closer*. A closer in the police department is a person who solves a crime and obtains confessions, and so, closes the case. In the series, Brenda Leigh Johnson is a Los Angeles Police Department Deputy Chief, who appears to close cases by whatever means necessary—with the mindset that the end justifies the means.

Imagine Jesus as our Closer when we've been victimized through manifold temptations, trials and tribulation. Jesus collared the perpetrator in the wilderness (Matthew 4:1-11)—the devil—and the case closed permanently through the final and ultimate work of His blood shed for our forgiveness (Hebrews 7:26-27). The case is not only closed through His victory in the wilderness, but through the cross and the resurrection, making it very possible to not be victimized in the first place.

Jesus is the Author and Finisher of our faith (Hebrews 12:1-2)—the Authorizer Who validates and legalizes our faith, and the Closer Who is the great "Amen" of our faith for every area of our lives.

In the book of Joshua there are two mistakes common to all of us. In Joshua 7, we find that after scouting the land and assured that it could be taken, the Israelites were defeated by the people of Ai—chased home. Joshua falls prostrate before the Lord to inquire as to why this thing has happened.

God's response is surprising: "Get up! Why are you lying there?" God tells Joshua, "This is not praying time, this is time for action," and proceeds to give Joshua instructions for rooting out the cause of their defeat.

Achan, from the tribe of Judah was the issue. He'd stolen gold, clothing and silver from the last battle knowing that it was forbidden to take *anything*. For this, Achan and his entire family were stoned.

There are times when prayer is an exercise in futility. It's time to *do* something. There was sin in the camp and God wanted the sin dealt with. What are you still praying about that you should be *doing*? Get up, take the directions you've been given and let's go!

In Joshua 9, the script flips. Joshua makes a move before inquiring of the Lord. The Gibeonites were scared to death of the Israelites, so they dressed in old clothes and toted stale bread, deceiving Joshua about who they were and why they were there. Joshua goes by external appearances and believing they were from a distant land, made a treaty with them. When he discovered who they really were, it was too late. In his integrity, he keeps his word to avoid more trouble with the Lord.

We often assume that how the Lord worked in one instance is the way He will work in other instances. No. It is therefore so important to keep an open ear and open heart to the Holy Spirit for guidance and direction in every matter. And, yes, as we learn at the feet of Jesus, it can be confusing. Like the new wife who told her husband as she set dinner in front of him, "Honey, I only make two dishes: cherry cheesecake and spaghetti," to which her husband replied, "Okay, dear. Just one question—which one is this?"

Just when we are at our wit's end with loose ends all over the place, Jesus steps in to enable us to solve the case and bring it to a close. He makes us aware of the enemy's strategies. In the case of Joshua, the scenario in chapter seven could be called an overt operation—it was obvious that the defeat was due to some breach and needed to be rooted out. In chapter nine, the strategy was a covert operation—the Gibeonites came incognito and Joshua made the mistake of judging a book by its cover.

Special Ops

In the case of the Lord Jesus Christ, the enemy boldly—overtly—approaches. It is a dual of words designed to ultimately abort the mission of redemption and dethrone Jesus as *the* one and only Son of God, Lord and Savior of the world. Covertly, the enemy went undercover attempting intimidation through the word "if" — "*if* You are the Son of God," or better translated, "*since* You are the Son of God." He was hoping Jesus had an ego that would cause Him to supersede the will of the Father.

The devil does not want us to have Jesus as Lord of our lives. He does not want us to have fellowship with Jesus. And, he doesn't want us to worship Jesus. Through His finished work on the cross and in the resurrection, Jesus secured all this for us. However, the enemy still works through temptation to entice us to choose to *not* do these things.

What if we get fooled into giving in? If Jesus is not Lord of all then He's not Lord at all and we limit His ability to do all that He needs to do and all that we desire Him to do *because* He is not Lord of our lives (Matthew 6:33). If we have no relationship with Christ, He then becomes a distant entity, uninterested in my wellbeing. Ignorable. If we do not worship Him, we miss the ability to draw His manifest presence and experience His majesty. In other words, the devil is saying that we should not be committed to Christ, have no communion with Christ and don't celebrate Christ.

God's Word is our lifeline and in every temptation, the enemy wants us to question the authority, the authenticity, the accuracy, the accountability and the aim of God's Word:

To tempt God means to believe He would lead you to a place where He would not provide for you, especially when He's already told you that He would. We do that when we question God's special presence among us (Christ in us); question

God's special providence for us (God's plans for us); question God's special promise to us (God comes through).

Authorization Needed

A few years ago, I'd asked my congregation to pray for me, but I didn't give any details. Here's what happened. I'd been in Dallas and heard a popular pastor on the hip-hop drive station doing an inspirational moment. I thought to myself, *I can do that! Give a shout-out to all the young people.* So, I put a package together which included some sample audio clips and a prospectus for the number one hip hop station in Chicago.

I talked to someone who had connections to the station. He took everything and pitched it. Not interested. But, I didn't give up. Here's how God works things out in His time and in His way.

A year later, I was at Salem Baptist Church of Chicago to bring the message. I was introduced in an unusual way. "We want to introduce Pastor Ford. Around here, we call him the 'love doctor.'" My sermon was on relationships. One of the members happened to work at the station to which I had submitted the clips and prospectus. Unbeknownst to me, they'd been discussing having a program that speaks to relationships on that station. She requested my CDs and books and took them to the station. I got a call from her saying the station was interested.

Point? God has a timetable—a calendar—for when He wants things done. It's a perfect timetable. Anything we try to do to help God out, will only make things worse and cause delays. Remember Abraham and Sarah? But, when it is God's time, He'll take care of it even though we don't have a clue as to what He's doing.

Now, the rest of the story. My publisher, *Lift Every Voice*, wanted me—as one of their most popular writers—to go on that station to do a two-minute interview. What time? Eight o'clock in the morning. I thought it through. I take care of my mother-in-law and my wife. I have my devotional time. I have to make breakfast. I'd have to get someone to come in to help.

Then, we're talking a drive downtown in rush hour traffic and pay to park for a two-minute interview. I offered to do the interview on the phone. No. Not gonna work. Must be face-to-face. No. No can do. I told the station, "No."

Then I got a call from my publisher. "We've never asked anything of you. We've published three of your books. We really need you to do this interview." They got me. Okay.

I arrived around 7:30am, only to discover the interview was at 8:30am not 8am. The atmosphere was not exactly charged up. But once the interview started, folks in the studio perked up and interacted. A two-minute interview stretched into fifteen minutes! It was like old home week. They realized how long the interview had lasted and felt obligated to play some music. I was invited back.

Later on, I got a call. The program director heard the interview and asked about me and whether I'd be interested in doing a program. The rest, as they say, is history. I am now the *Love Doctor* at Inspiration 1390 AM Chicago.

Look at what God did. When I thought I should have done this, nothing happened. It wasn't God's time, nor was it God's way. Two years later, without any assistance from me, God set it up. I wasn't even going! BUT GOD! And no one could get the glory on this thing except God.

God knew what He wanted and when and how to broker and close the deal. God gets me the greatest blessing, for the greatest good, for the greatest number of people, for His greatest glory. And, with the least amount of worry and hassle.

Validation Without Authorization

The devil takes Jesus to the pinnacle of the temple. This would be the southeast corner of Herod's Royal Portico. This is *not* the temple Solomon built. Nebuchadnezzar destroyed that with the exception of Solomon's Porch, which was also located in the same area as the pinnacle. There is a breathtaking view of the Kidron Valley from that pinnacle, which has a 450–700ft drop.

In rabbinic literature, the Midrash states the Jewish belief that the Messiah would make himself known by standing on the roof of the temple - the pinnacle. Was part of this temptation to get Jesus to fulfill Malachi 3:1 before the God's time?

The devil challenges Jesus' Sonship once more. He dares Jesus to dive off the pinnacle of the temple, misquoting Psalm 91:11–12 for God's protection in doing so. Now, let me say this: God protects His people. Hebrews 1:14 tells us we have angels covering us on God's command, not ours. Stories abound in the Bible and in the testimonies of others concerning God's protection.

Running on God!

A woman is on her way to her car in the mall parking lot. Her car is the only car left. She notices two men moving toward her and she does not have a good feeling about it. She hurriedly gets into her car and tries to start it but it won't start. She prays urgently, "Oh, God! You've got to get me out of here!" She tries again and the car starts. She pulls off quickly.

She gets home and collapses in thanksgiving to God because she knew what they had on their minds. She leaves the next morning headed to work and the car refused to start. She called the mechanic to tow her car. It worked last night but not this morning. The mechanic picked the car up and called her later.

"That car didn't work last night," the mechanic informed her.

"But it did work," she insisted, "because I drove it home." She told him the story of the two men and God answering her prayer.

"Well, if God started your car," he retorted, "He did it without a battery because your car does not have a battery in it!"

The Locksmith

Dr. David Jeremiah tells the story of having locked his keys in the car and couldn't get in to retrieve them. He was using a coat hanger to try to trip the lock when a guy walked up—big, burly. It was scary.

"You havin' problems?" the guy asked.

"Yeah," Dr. Jeremiah answered. "We have an emergency and I can't get into my car. Can you help me?"

"Yeah, I can help ya." The guy *boomp, boomps* on the door and it unlocks!

"Wow! You're a Godsend!" Dr. Jeremiah exclaimed incredulously.

"Well, I don't know about that. I just got out of prison yesterday," he said.

"What were you in prison for?"

"Car theft." Dr. Jeremiah stopped and prayed right there. Not only did God send help—He sent a professional!

So, yes, God protects us in both awesome and ordinary ways. We all have stories of God's intervention to protect us and even save our lives. The problem in Jesus' wilderness experience on that pinnacle is that the devil was trying to entice Jesus to do what? Yes! Put God to the test. To tempt God by taking unauthorized action—an action against the will of God, and he was twisting the Scriptures to justify it. He wanted Jesus to validate His Godship without authorization from the Father, which he already knew would not work.

Theologian John Phillips says this on the pinnacle issue:

> "This is what the devil is saying to Jesus, 'Jesus, You aren't going anywhere. Here you are thirty years of age and You have no audience, no followers, no acclaim. You're not even known. 'If You listen to me and do what I say You can be famous instantly! A celebrity overnight. Your name will be on everybody's lips. You'll be on front page news. I'll see that you get the crowds.
>
> 'Now, here's the plan: I'll set You up here on the pinnacle of the temple. You can't get any higher than

that in Jerusalem. The people down there in the
temple courts look as small as ants.

'Look! You've already attracted their attention. In a
moment, You can have their applause. You are now
where You should have been years ago—in the public eye.
Now that I have brought you up, You cast Yourself down.'"

What is the devil saying here? "You must do something dar-
ing. Something spectacular. You say You trust Your Heavenly Father? Well, prove it! Exercise your faith. Cast Yourself
down.

"Okay, Jesus, You're being tested, now *You* put God to the
test." That's something we really don't want to do. And Jesus
acknowledges that we don't want to put God to the test (Matthew 4:7). This is certainly not trusting God—this is tempting God.

What do we learn? He has Jesus on the pinnacle of the temple. He can persuade us, but he can't push us. You and I need
to realize that the devil creates the temptation, but we create
the transgression.

> *Let no man say when he is tempted, I am tempted of God:*
> *for God cannot be tempted with evil, neither tempteth he*
> *any man: but every man is tempted, when he is drawn*
> *away of his own lust, and enticed. Then when lust hath*
> *conceived, it bringeth forth sin: and sin, when it is*
> *finished, bringeth forth death.*
> *Do not err, my beloved brethren.*
> ***James 1:13-16***

Arrogant Authority

Here is what we want to be careful of: being one of those people who tells God what to do, when to do it and how to do it. Who puts time constraints on God. Who says, "If You are God and You are good, You will." I dare say that most of us have gone that route at some time. I know I did when my mother was on her deathbed.

I think of it as the audacity of authority where we take the promises of God and take the faith that He's given to us and think that we can tell God what to do. Now, we already said this—what trumps our faith? Yes! The sovereignty of God. Even though we have the faith, if it's not in God's plan, He trumps your faith with His sovereignty. He says, "Yes, you do believe. You do have faith. But I have a different plan. And giving you this now, in this way, does not fit in My plan."

Imagine the story of the DEA agent who visited a ranch for inspection. He showed the rancher his ID and proceeded. The rancher stopped him to warn him:

"Just don't go into that section of the field over there because—"

"Shut up!" the agent spat out. "This badge says I am a DEA agent and I have the authority of the United States government behind me! You see this badge? I can go anywhere I want, no questions asked, no answers given!" and with that, he proceeded to conduct his inspection.

The rancher went on to do chores. Shortly, the agent was seen running for his life with the rancher's prize bull in hot pursuit. "Help!" the agent screamed.

Yelled the rancher as the agent got closer, "Show 'im your badge!"

Who else might be prone to get tempted with undue authority? A novice. Someone who is young in salvation, in faith, in experience, in wisdom... This person would be prone to pride and falling into the devil's traps (1 Timothy 3:6).

The connotation of the word "novice" is that of a newly planted tree. What's the basic characteristic of a newly planted tree? Easy to pull up by the roots. A fully matured tree? Not easy to do—unmovable. Rooted.

Evidence!

Son of man, take up a lamentation upon the king of Tyrus, and say unto him, Thus saith the Lord God; Thou sealest up the sum, full of wisdom, and perfect in beauty. Thou hast been in Eden the garden of God; every precious stone was thy covering, the sardius, topaz, and the diamond, the beryl, the onyx, and the jasper, the sapphire, the emerald, and the carbuncle, and gold: the workmanship of thy tabrets and of thy pipes was prepared in thee in the day that thou wast created. Thou art the anointed cherub that covereth; and I have set thee so: thou wast upon the holy mountain of God; thou hast walked up and down in the midst of the stones of fire. Thou wast perfect in thy ways from the day that thou wast created, till iniquity was found in thee. By the multitude of thy merchandise they have filled the midst of thee with violence, and thou hast sinned: therefore I will cast thee as profane out of the mountain of God: and I will destroy thee, O covering cherub, from the midst of

WHAT TO DO WHEN THE DEVIL TALKS TO YOU

*the stones of fire. Thine heart was lifted up because of
thy beauty, thou hast corrupted thy wisdom by reason
of thy brightness: I will cast thee to the ground, I will
lay thee before kings, that they may behold thee. Thou
hast defiled thy sanctuaries by the multitude of thine
iniquities, by the iniquity of thy traffick; therefore will
I bring forth a fire from the midst of thee, it shall devour
thee, and I will bring thee to ashes upon the earth in
the sight of all them that behold thee. All they that know
thee among the people shall be astonished at thee: thou
shalt be a terror, and never shalt thou be any more.*
Ezekiel 28:12-19

Attempted Identity Theft

*How art thou fallen from heaven, O Lucifer, son of the
morning! how art thou cut down to the ground, which
didst weaken the nations!
For thou hast said in thine heart,
I will ascend into heaven,
I will exalt my throne above the stars of God:
I will sit also upon the mount of the congregation,
in the sides of the north:
I will ascend above the heights of the clouds;
I will be like the most High.*
Isaiah 14:12-14

But all these things were fulfilled in Christ Jesus because He
is the real One, the Creator, the Owner:

> *I WILL ASCEND INTO HEAVEN*
> **Ephesians 4:8-10**
> *Therefore He says:*

"When He ascended on high, He led captivity captive, and gave gifts to men." (Now this, "He ascended"—what does it mean but that He also first descended into the lower parts of the earth? He who descended is also the One who ascended far above all the heavens, that He might fill all things.)

I WILL EXALT MY THRONE ABOVE THE STARS OF GOD
Ephesians 1:20-22
He worked in Christ when He raised Him from the dead and seated Him at His right hand in the heavenly places, far above all principality and power and might and dominion, and every name that is named, not only in this age but also in that which is to come. And He put all things under His feet, and gave Him to be head over all things to the church, which is His body, the fullness of Him who fills all in all.

I WILL SIT ALSO UPON THE MOUNT OF THE CONGREGATION, IN THE SIDES OF THE NORTH
Hebrews 5:5-6
So also Christ glorified not himself to be made an high priest; but he that said unto him, Thou art my Son, to day have I begotten thee. As he saith also in another place, Thou art a priest for ever after the order of Melchisedec.

I WILL ASCEND ABOVE THE HEIGHTS OF THE CLOUDS
Hebrews 5:26
For such a High Priest was fitting for us, who is holy, harmless, undefiled, separate from sinners, and has

become higher than
the heavens...

I WILL BE LIKE THE MOST HIGH.
Hebrews 1:2-6
[God] hath in these last days spoken unto us by his Son,
whom he hath appointed heir of all things, by whom
also he made the worlds; Who being the brightness
of his glory, and the express image of his person, and
upholding all things by the word of his power, when he
had by himself purged our sins, sat down on the right
hand of the Majesty on high: Being made so much better
than the angels, as he hath by inheritance obtained a
more excellent name than they.

For unto which of the angels said he at any time,
Thou art my Son, this day have I begotten thee? And
again, I will be to him a Father, and he shall be to
me a Son? And again, when he bringeth in the
firstbegotten into the world, he saith, And let all the
angels of God worship him.

CASE CLOSED.

And so. What do we do when the devil talks to us?
Listen to Jesus.

If anyone has ears to hear, let him hear!"
Mark 7:16

ABOUT THE AUTHOR

MARANATHA!

Dr. James Ford Jr. and his wife Leslie have been serving the Lord at Christ Bible Church of Chicago (formerly South Shore Baptist Church), located on the south side of Chicago, Illinois, for 32 years. They have been married 45 years and have three sons, James III (Tenille), Nathaniel (who went home to be with the Lord November 26, 1999) and Jonathan (MeShanda). They also have nine grandchildren.

Pastor Ford is a graduate of Moody Bible Institute and completed his Master's degree at Trinity Evangelical Divinity School. He has served on several boards, including the Baptist General Conference's Board of World Missions and the Board of Overseers, Board of Directors of the Ada S. McKinley Special Educational Services, Board of Directors of Fellowship Christian Academy, and the Alumni Board of Moody Bible Institute. In 2015, St. Thomas University in St. Thomas,

Florida, conferred an honorary doctorate on Pastor, now Dr. James Ford, Jr.

Pastor Ford is the senior pastor of Christ Bible Church of Chicago as well as the president of Impact Ministries, which is an outreach ministry of Christ Bible Church committed to strengthening families in the South Shore Community of Chicago. He provides the messages for Impact Ministries' radio broadcasts, "Treasured Truth for Troubling Times," which is aired daily over WMBI AM-1110 and WMBI 90.1-FM, as well as over 160 WMBI syndicate and affiliate stations nationwide and in some U.S. territories. Pastor Ford is featured twice a week on Gospel Radio 1390 AM.

Honored as "Pastor of the Year" (1993) by Moody Bible Institute, Pastor Ford has been a speaker at Moody Bible Institute's annual Founder's Week and is a contributor in the book, *A Heart for the City*, published by Moody Press. He is an international conference speaker, seminar leader, and author. His first book, *When a Man Loves a Woman,* was published in July 2004, followed by *Seven Reasons Why God Created Marriage* in October 2009, *When A Woman Loves a Man* in 2011, *Living the Blessed Life* in 2015, and in 2016 *A New Look At An Old Prayer* was released. Pastor Ford has been an Adjunct Professor at Moody Bible Institute, an instructor for the Pacific Garden Mission's Bible program in Chicago, Illinois and is a special instructor at Ecola Bible School in Cannon Beach, Oregon. Currently, Dr. Ford serves on the board of trustees for Pacific Garden Mission in Chicago.

Through his strong passion for building up the body of Christ through the expository preaching and teaching of the

Word of God (Col. 1:28), Pastor Ford's work supports Christian marriages and helps believers see marriage as God intended. He is above all else a lover of Jesus Christ, submitted to His Lordship.

To order more copies of this book or to contact Pastor Ford for speaking engagements, please visit: *www.jfordjr.com* and *www.christbiblechurchofchicago.org*.